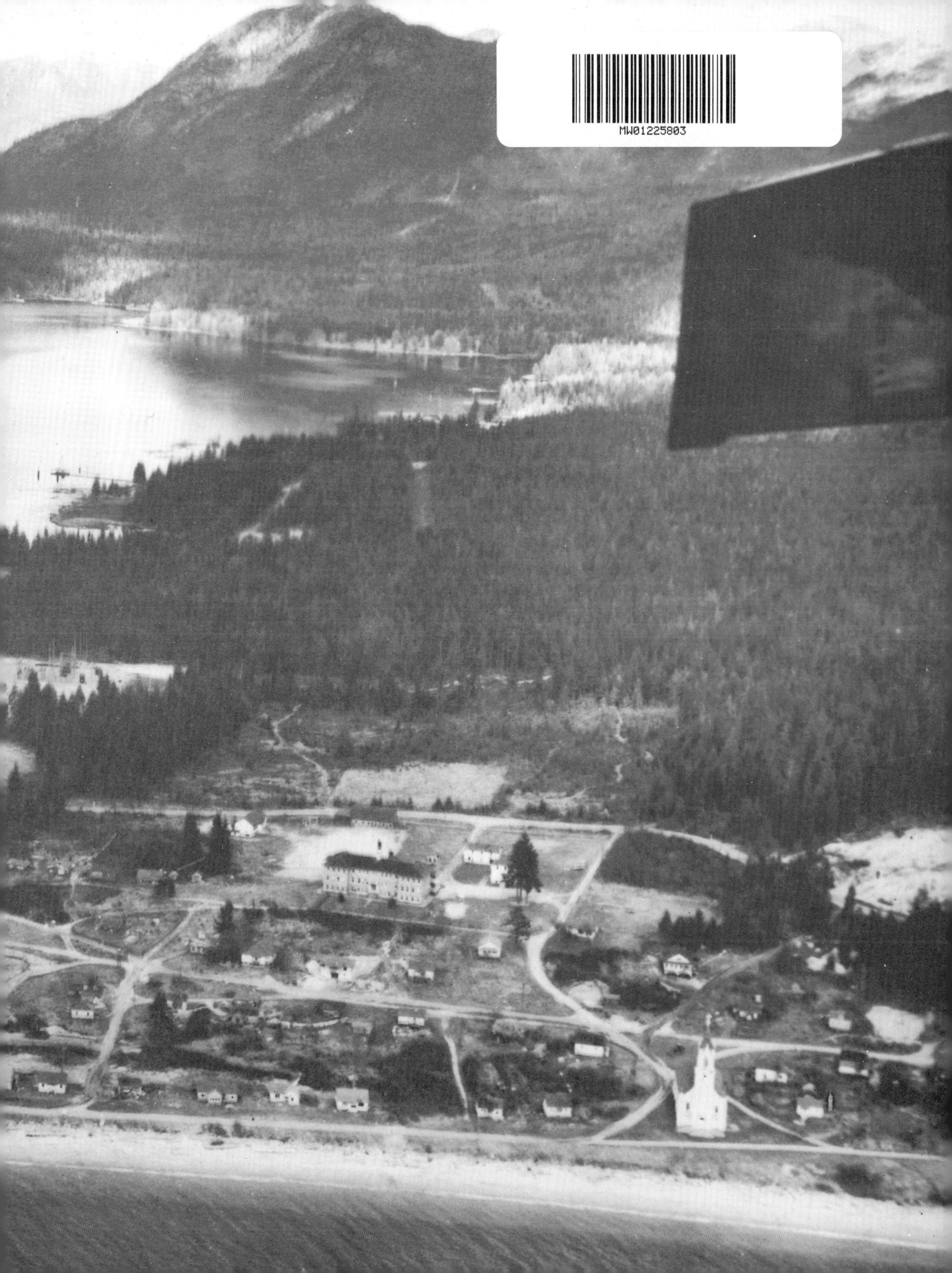

HELEN DAWE'S
SECHELT

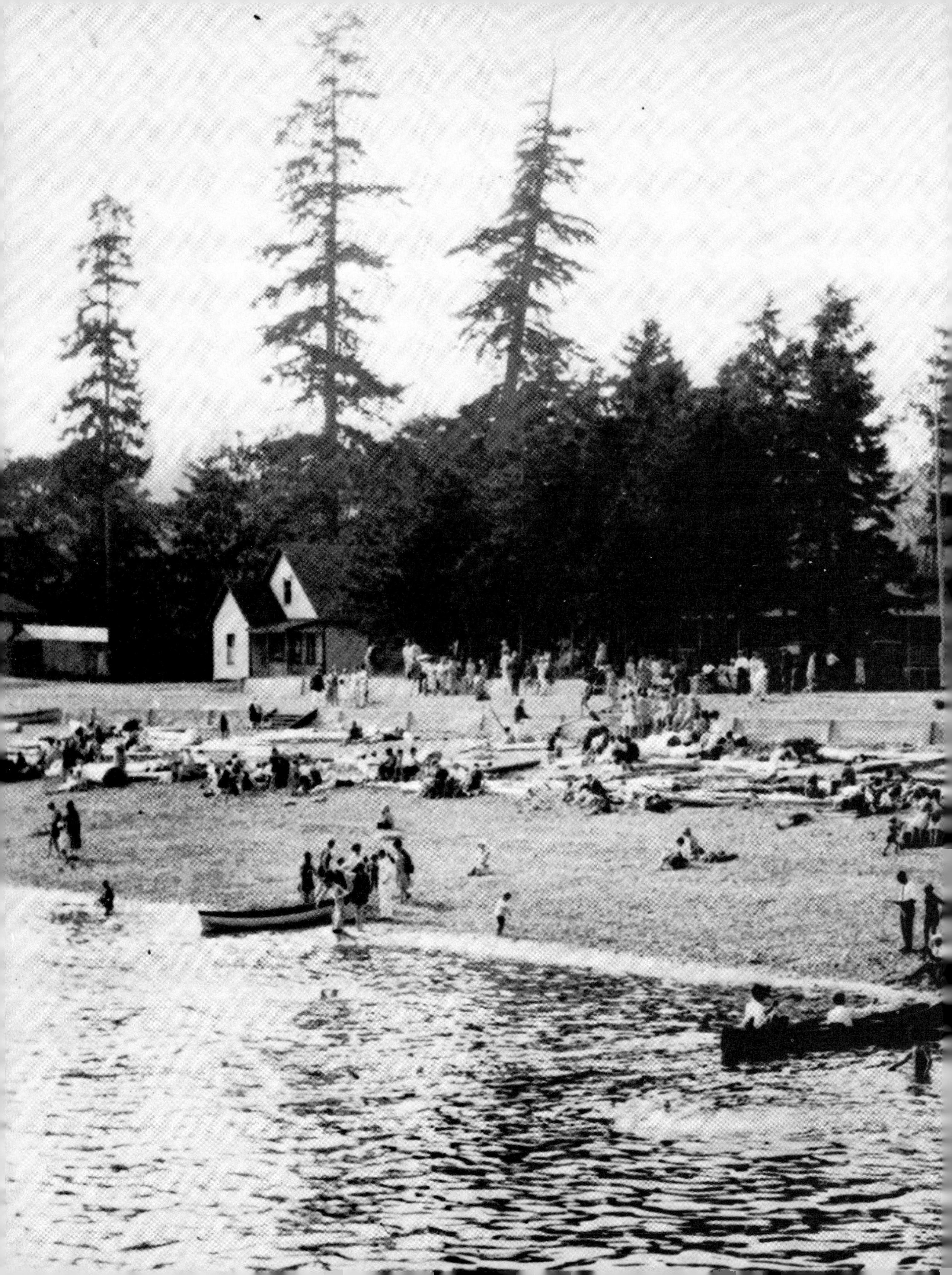

HELEN DAWE'S
SECHELT

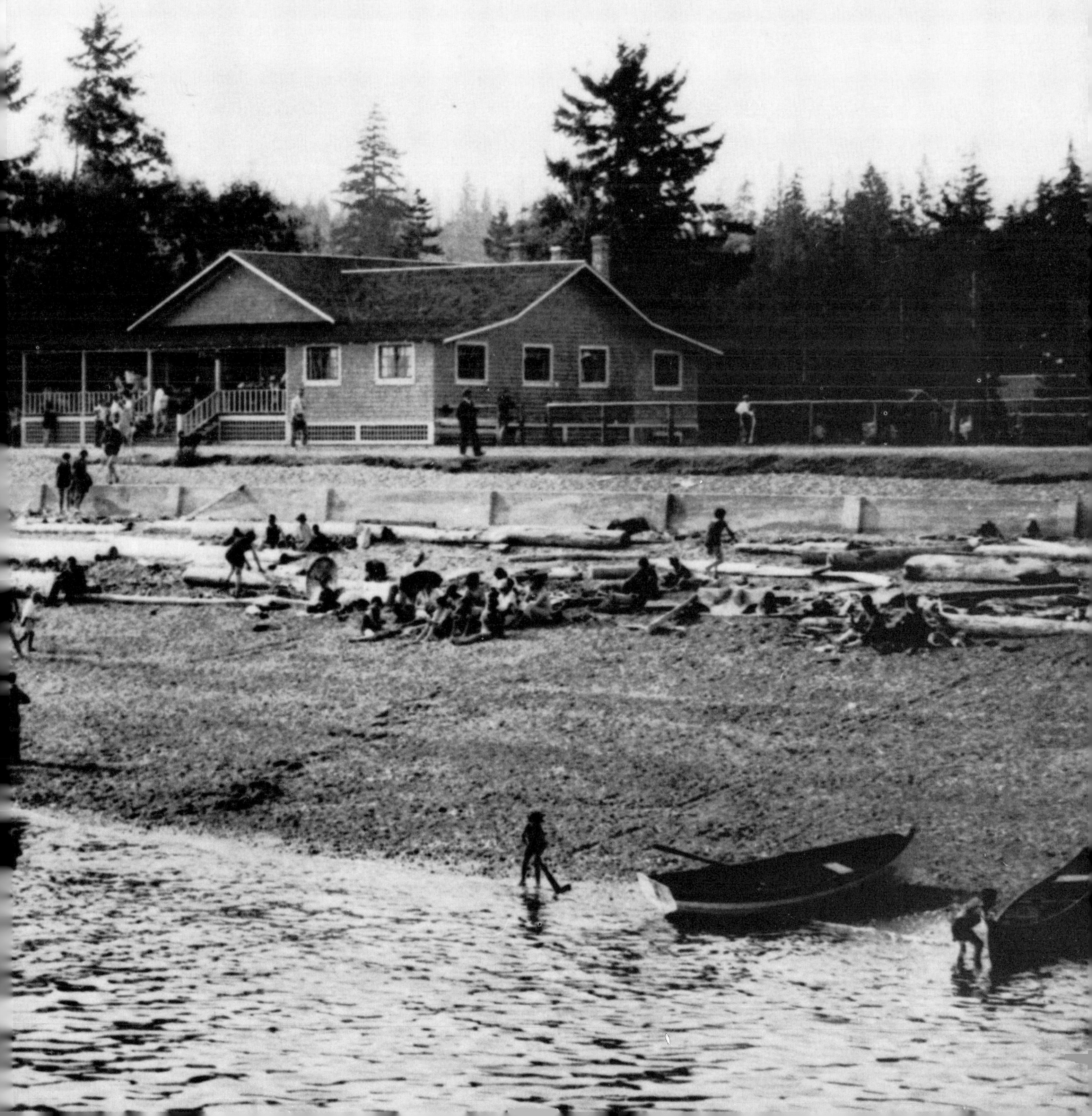

Harbour Publishing
P.O. Box 219
Madeira Park, BC Canada V0N 2H0

Edited by Alec Macaulay
Jacket painting *Sechelt in 1902* by Henry J. De Forest (1860–1924)
Design by Roger Handling
Printed and bound in Canada by Friesen Printers

Canadian Cataloguing in Publication Data

Dawe, Helen, 1914–1983
Helen Dawe's Sechelt

ISBN 1-55017-027-9
1. Sechelt (B.C.)—History.   2.Sechelt (B.C.)—Biography.   3. Dawe, Helen, 1914–1983.
I. Title.
FC3849.S43D39 1990   971.1′31   C90-091599-4
F1089.5.S43D39 1990

CONTENTS

Irvine Ck.
TUWANEK
Carlson Ck.
Gray Ck.
SECHELT INLET
N
Angus Ck.
Burnet Ck.
Kenyon Ck.
Wakefield Ck.
PORPOISE BAY
Chapman Ck.
SECHELT
SARGEANT BAY
TRAIL BAY
SELMA PARK
DAVIS BAY
Wilson Ck.
WILSON CREEK
TRAIL ISLANDS
Flume Ck.
Clack Ck.
Roberts Ck.
STRAIT OF GEORGIA
WHITE ISLAND
ROBERTS CREEK

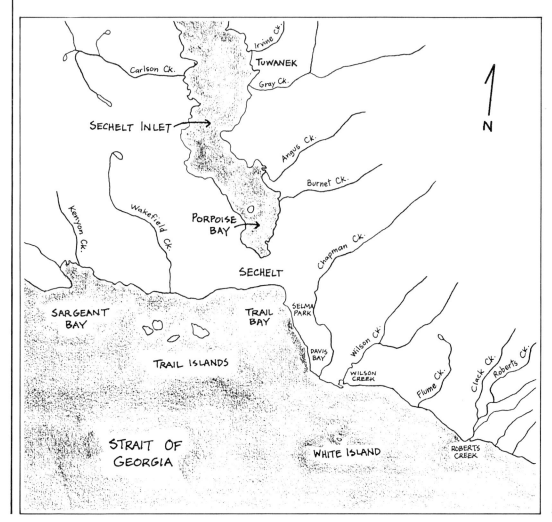

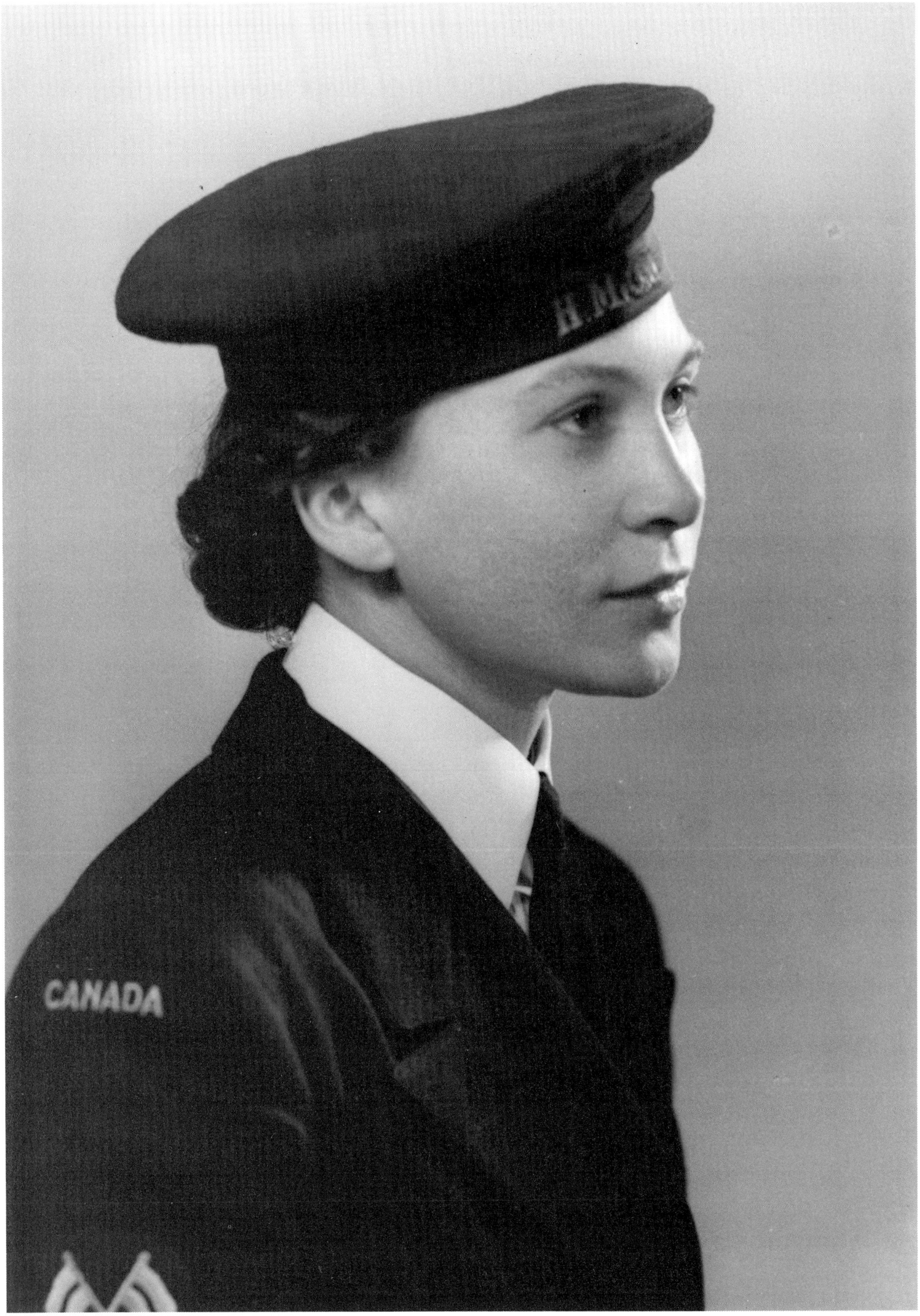
CANADA

FOREWORD

Helen Dawe had a lifelong interest in study and learning—the student's desire to know, to find out what is here in the world.

She had many interests and a life of varied experiences, including overseas service in the Royal Canadian Navy and work as a librarian in the US Air Force and the Vancouver Public Library.

But an ongoing project throughout her sixty-nine years was the assembling of writings, photographs, artifacts and community records of the people and events of her place and time.

Her place was the village of Sechelt, where her grandfather, Thomas John Cook, first visited in 1891 and then settled with his family in 1894. She grew up during a time when many of the settlement's original pioneers were still living, and when the stories of the community's building were still fresh in their memories. She listened to these stories, and through her research uncovered others. She filed and annotated the items she collected with great diligence and care, and the result of her work is a well-organized and diverse assemblage of memorabilia covering roughly the last one hundred years of Sechelt's development.

It is also important to realize that Helen was as concerned about ensuring Sechelt's future as she was about preserving its past. She keenly observed, for instance, every village council meeting, and was determined that the community which her family was instrumental in founding should not be spoiled for those who might live there in years to come. It was for the benefit of those future residents of Sechelt, as well as in tribute to its early settlers, that she conducted her work.

Although she never found the time to compile the book (or books) she intended to write "someday," she did select topical photographs from her collection and annotate these with extended captions. These were published from time to time in local newspapers. She also wrote occasional pieces on topics of timely application as events transpired.

This book offers some of these recollections as a memorial of her work and life in this village for which she had an enduring affection.

Helen was born in Vancouver on December 23, 1914, and died at Sechelt on December 28, 1983.

BILLIE STEELE
(sister of Helen Dawe)
EARL DAWE
(cousin of Helen Dawe)

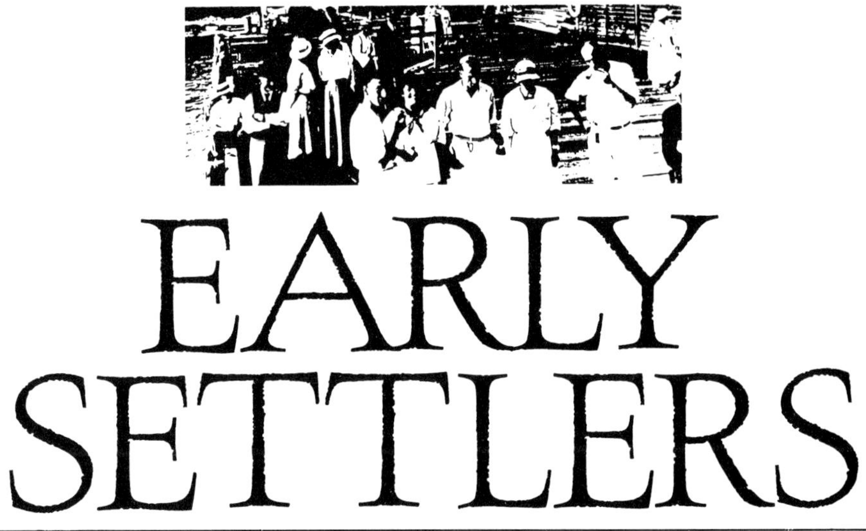

EARLY SETTLERS

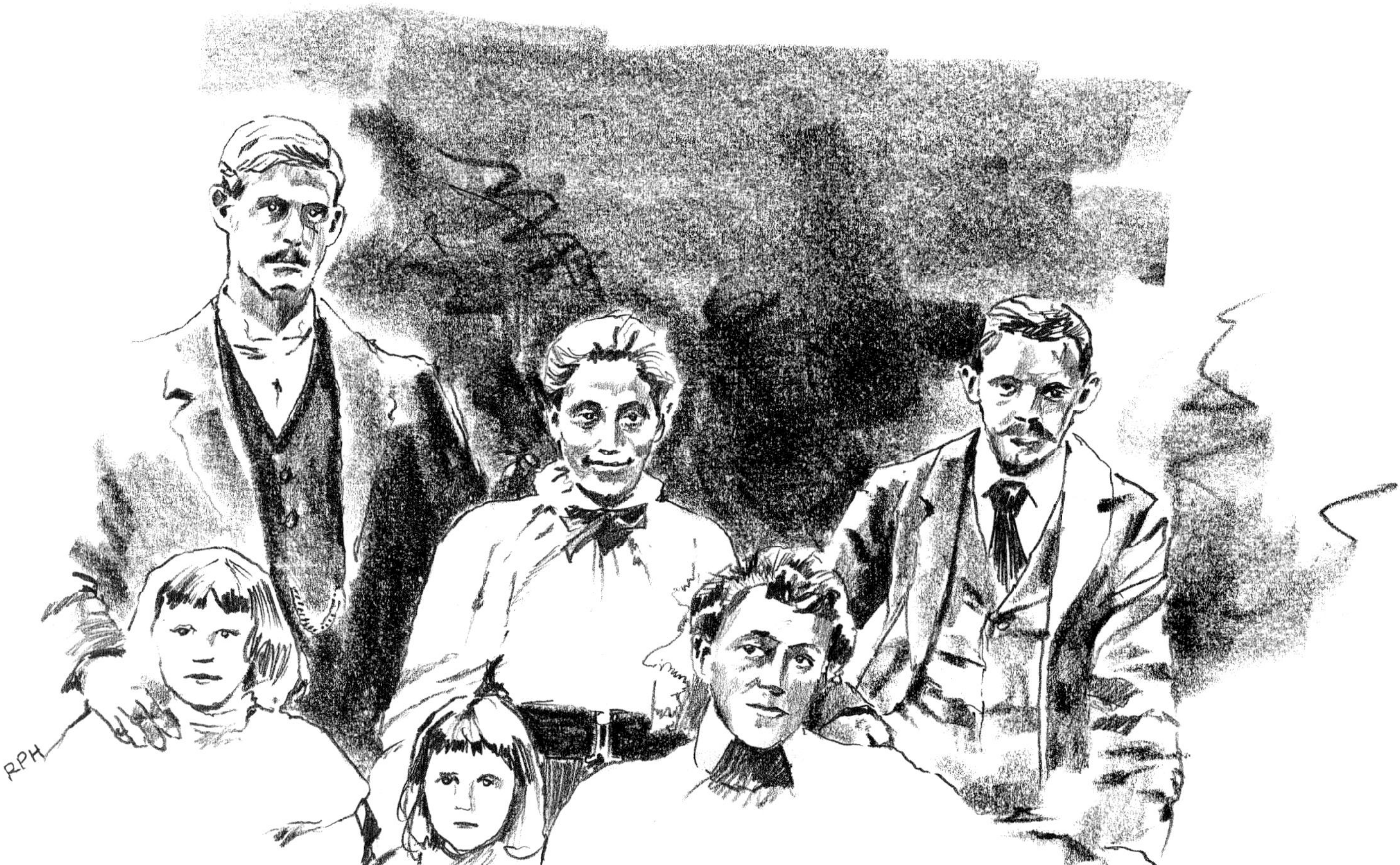
RPH

JOHN SCALES AND THE FIRST LAND SURVEYS OF SECHELT

TWO YEARS before British Columbia became a province of Canada, John Scales, the founding father of the white settlement at Sechelt, wrote a letter from New Westminster on May 25, 1869 to the Honourable J.W. Trutch, chief commissioner of lands and works for the Colony of British Columbia. Mr. Scales' letter begged leave to locate the 150-acre military land grant, to which he was entitled after serving in the Royal Engineers, on crown land lying between Trail Bay and Porpoise Bay, now the heart of the Corporation of Sechelt. His military grant to District Lot 303 on Trail Bay was recorded May 25, 1869. His purchase of District Lot 304—the adjoining 110 acres on Porpoise Bay—began on July 17, 1875. Sechelt Indian Reserve No. 2, immediately to the east, was not allotted until December 1876.

Scales, a Yorkshireman, had arrived in New Westminster in April 1859 as a sapper with the main contingent of the Royal Engineers. A sapper was a soldier employed in saps or making trenches, the equivalent of a private in rank. He, his wife Mary Sarah, their eldest son John Henry and their first daughter Elizabeth

The original application, including a rough map, for 150 acres between Porpoise Bay and Trail Bay, made by John Scales in 1869.

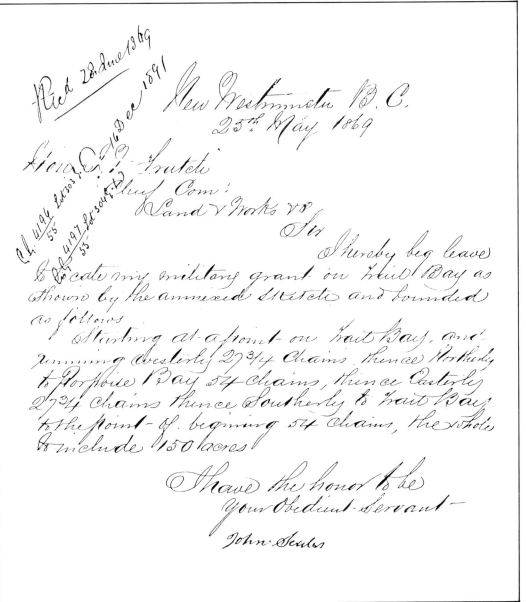

had travelled aboard the clipper ship *Thames City* from England by way of Cape Horn, a six-month journey. The two children were born in 1854 and 1857 respectively on the Island of Mauritius in the Indian Ocean, where their father served with the Royal Engineers until he contracted cholera and was invalided home.

The corps of Royal Engineers aided in bringing law and order to the infant colony of BC. At that time, in the 1850s, gold had been discovered along the Fraser and an estimated twenty-five thousand people, some of questionable reputation, had flocked to the area. Troops of the Royal Engineers assisted with the Gold Escort. The commanding officer, Colonel R.C. Moody, arrived in Victoria on Christmas day in 1858 via the Isthmus of Panama, and he was later to select John Scales as his batman or orderly.

Historian David Veitch has described the state of the northwest that Scales arrived at in 1857: "The mainland of BC was at that time merely a vast fur preserve of the Hudson's Bay Company. Inhabited by less than a score of white men scattered among a dozen or so widely separated trading posts of the company, it was a complete wilderness without government, towns, roads or means of transportation."

The special detachment of the British Royal Engineers remained in BC as a corps for only five years, leaving before the colony of Vancouver Island was incorporated into the mainland colony of BC in 1866. During that time, however, they made the first surveys, built the first roads and bridges and laid out many of today's cities and towns. They prepared and published the first maps, and designed the first postage stamps. They established the first churches, the first schoolhouses, the first permanent observatory, the first private hospital and the first library. The Royal Engineers' press printed books as well as the first *BC Gazette*. They built their barracks, married

quarters, auxiliary structures and a theatre at Sapperton near New Westminster, then the capital of the colony. In 1864 the first session of the first legislative council of BC opened in what had been the barracks of the Royal Engineers, so in effect they erected the first parliament buildings.

William Sugden Jemmett, who conducted the first legal survey of Sechelt in 1875, seen here in 1879.

Colonel Moody's detachment was selected from a large number of volunteers. The men were attracted in part by the promise of thirty acres of free land after six years' service in BC. This was later increased to 150 acres after five years. Every man in the BC detachment had to be a tradesman, chosen on the basis of including all occupations which might be useful in establishing the new colony. John Scales, who worked at his trade as a stonemason or stonecutter while on active service in the colony, must have felt at home when he observed the granite bluffs abounding on the Sunshine Coast, but he was wise enough to choose for himself the key flat land on the Sechelt Isthmus, the natural transportation route and portage for men going up the Sechelt Inlet in the early days.

In 1863 Britain disbanded the detachment of Royal Engineers serving in British Columbia. Officers and men were given the choice of returning to England or remaining in the colony as settlers. All of the officers and twenty of the men went home, but the remaining 130, including Scales, stayed in BC to earn their keep in civilian life. Many worked in various building trades, a few as architects; others contributed as surveyors, tailors, shoemakers, blacksmiths, undertakers, bookkeepers, photographers and hotel keepers.

The year 1875 is significant in the development of Sechelt, for it was then that Captain William Sugden Jemmett was employed to survey what subsequently became known as District Lots 303 and 304, lying across the isthmus between Trail and Porpoise Bays. When Captain Jemmett made the 1875 survey he knew that John Scales' original 1869 application included more than the 150 acres of free land to which his military service entitled him. The area was therefore divided into two district lots, the smaller of which had to be purchased by Scales. (In recent years the stump of one of Jemmett's 1875 bearing trees was discovered by Sechelt land surveyor Doug Roy. Carved into a blaze on the stump was the information "N 54 W, 26 L", indicating north 54 degrees west, distance 26 links.)

In August 1975 the Sechelt and District Chamber of Commerce issued a proclamation declaring it the year of the "Sechelt Centennial." Strictly speaking, they were six years out in their attempt at history because the official land records in Victoria date District Lot 303 from May 25, 1869. The year 1875 did mark the first legal survey in Sechelt, though prior to this there were prospectors ranging in the local hills searching for minerals. On November 6, 1873 three men, Jabez A. Culver, Neil McKinnon and James Laidlaw had applied for separate pre-emptions on Narrows Arm, Sechelt Inlet.

It was commonplace in the early days of the province for a man to wait many years before he took action to obtain the final Crown grant to land for which he might have applied much earlier. So it was not until December 16, 1891 that John Scales received from Queen Victoria his military grant to the 150 acres comprising District Lot 303, plus the Crown grant to 110 acres making up lot 304, for which he paid $110. The letters patent effecting these transactions bear the name of Hugh Nelson, lieutenant governor of BC.

While the facts are uncertain, historians suggest that Nelson and Scales may well have met when Scales worked for Moody, Dietz and Nelson's sawmill. In any event, it was not long after Scales received legal title that he sold his Sechelt properties to the Honourable Hugh Nelson. Nelson—for whom the community of Nelson and Nelson Street in Vancouver are named—was a member of the last colonial legislature of BC as well as the first Canadian Parliament. In 1879 he was named to the senate, and in 1887 was appointed the fourth lieutenant governor of BC. His term ended in 1892 and he and his wife left for England, where he died the following March. His widow, Emily, inherited the Sechelt properties, which she sold to Herbert Whitaker about 1895.

John Scales, the first white landowner on the Sunshine Coast, died in Nanaimo on July 13, 1906. Perhaps on a clear summer's day he had occasionally looked out from some point on Vancouver Island to observe the white twin towers of the Sechelt Indian church, Our Lady of the Rosary, shining from across the Strait.

THOMAS JOHN COOK

ON APRIL 5, 1894, the steam tug *Tepic* departed Vancouver, rounded Mission Point and proceeded toward the Trail Bay beach. She hove to in the small bay west of what is now the foot of Shorncliffe Avenue, Sechelt. Aboard the tug were Thomas John Cook, his wife Sarah Belle and their infant daughter Ada. These 11

three passengers became the first white family to take up residence in Sechelt and settle permanently, so that today four generations of John and Sarah Cook's descendants live on the peninsula. Previously there had only been transient loggers, prospectors, traders, missionaries and the like. The flat-bottomed *Tepic* towed a scow containing the Cook family's household furnishings. These were unloaded onto the beach and moved into a log house Mr. Cook had built prior to the family's arrival on District Lot 1331, which he had pre-empted in 1891. Later, Shorncliffe Avenue was named for Mr. Cook's subdivision, which in turn was named for a place in Kent near where Mr. Cook grew up.

The *Tepic* shown docked in Vancouver. It was constructed in England in 1883 for the French, who were digging the Panama Canal. They sold her to Evans, Coleman and Evans, who brought her to Vancouver in 1889, the first steel tug on the BC coast. The *Tepic* was decommissioned in 1938 after contributing greatly to the industrial history of our province.

Thomas John Cook and family in front of his second log house, built in 1894. The photo was taken in 1895. Left to right: Sarah Cook; Ada Cook (later Ada Dawe); T.J. Cook; two sons of Dick Spinks, lawyer, visiting from Vancouver.

T.J. Cook had come to Canada around 1883 at the age of nineteen, after working as a messenger in England for the exiled Empress Eugenie of France. Once in Canada he joined the staff of George Stephen, later Lord Mount Stephen, first president of the Canadian Pacific Railway. Cook left Stephen's employ in 1889, the year he married Sarah McLachlan in Montreal. After settling his family in Sechelt, from 1897 to 1907 he worked as a steward on Canadian Pacific's *Empress of India*, which travelled to China and Japan. Between visits to the Orient, Sechelt was home.

A view of the Trail Islands, the first hotel, part of the Indian village and the bog, circa 1900.

THE WHITAKER FAMILY AND OTHERS

BERT WHITAKER and his father Alfred had already pre-empted District Lot 1473 at Porpoise Bay on March 17, 1892 by the time the two of them arrived from England in 1893 to scout the area. The pre-emption occurred shortly after Bert's seventeenth birthday, In 1894 the whole family—including parents and seven young people—were reunited at Sechelt. By 1895, Bert was subdividing District Lots 303 and 304 to form "Seechelt Townsite" after purchasing the lots from the Nelson family. After becoming local postmaster on March 1, 1896, Bert Whitaker began assembling a minor empire which eventually included two hotels, a series of stores and two steamship companies. He also owned the local wharves, a couple of sawmills, five logging camps and a group of revenue cottages. It is not surprising that when Grace Kent arrived in the town in 1912 to teach school, she observed that Bert Whitaker "owned practically all of Sechelt." Whitaker Park and Whitaker Road in Davis Bay are named for Bert Whitaker's younger brother Ron, and Whitaker Beach, between Roberts Creek and Gibsons, was named for Bert's cousin, Arthur Whitaker. Another Whitaker cousin, Edric S.

Log house built by Thomas John Cook in 1894, Sechelt. On April 5, 1894 T.J. Cook brought his wife Sarah and his three-month-old daughter Ada, later Mrs. Sam Dawe, to live in this log house until he built a larger home later in the same year. They arrived on the tug *Tepic* with their household goods on a scow. Left to right: T.J. Cook, Sarah Cook, Dick Spinks, Ada Cook and Mrs. Ursula Ingalls, known then as Spinks. The house disappeared between 1904 and 1912.

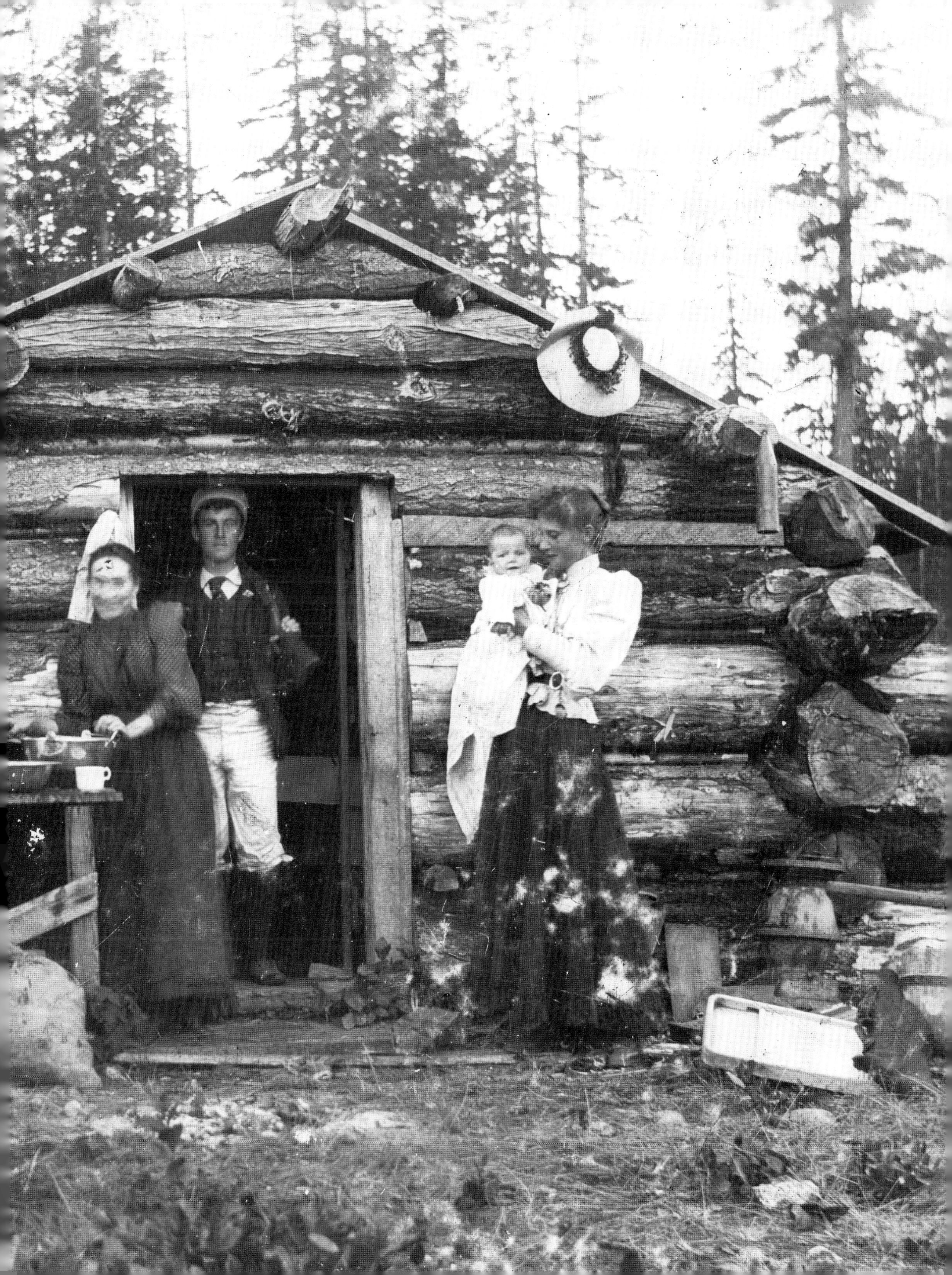

The view down Wharf Road in Sechelt, circa 1906–1910, shows a rear view of Sechelt pioneer Bert Whitaker's buildings facing Trail Bay on the Boulevard. The broad ditch on the east side of what was then called Porpoise Bay Road was made to drain the bog; it was not part of the mythic "canal" between Trail Bay and Porpoise Bay. Buildings left to right are: (1) third store and post office, erected in 1906 and destroyed by fire in July 1936; (2) wharf shed; (3) first Sechelt store and post office; (4) second store and post office—became the first Sechelt school in 1912; (5) first Sechelt hotel, opened July 1, 1899 and destroyed by fire in 1914.

Clayton, came to Sechelt after the First World War to work in the family enterprises. He managed the Union company's store on the waterfront from 1928 to 1949 and in 1950 opened Clayton's Self-Service Grocery on Cowrie Street. In 1956 the name was changed to Tom Boy store, and later it became a member of the Shop-Easy chain.

Some of the early pioneers worked with or for the Whitaker family. Pete Le Vesque, who lived at Porpoise Bay and was one of the first white men to live in Sechelt, once shared a shack with Bert Whitaker. "French Pete," as he was often called, was born in Canada of French ancestors, and was known to have occasionally led the patrons at the Sechelt

One of Sechelt's pioneer families, the Whitakers, on the Trail Bay shingle in front of their home, Beach House, during the first decade of the twentieth century. Alfred and his wife Henrietta built Beach House about 1905–06 on land which now accommodates the Driftwood Inn on the Boulevard. Note the natural shoreline before the still-extant wooden bulwark was built in 1926. Some of the pictured are, left to right: Front row: three of Henrietta's children, Evelyn Whitaker (later Mrs. Jack Haslett), Muriel Whitaker (later Mrs. Norman Thompson) and Ronald Whitaker. Back row: Horace J. Haslett, who married Evelyn in 1907, Mrs. Henrietta Julia Whitaker, Herbert Whitaker and Alfred Whitaker.

Hotel saloon in a round of dancing and singing. He sometimes worked for Bert Whitaker at jobs such as cutting wood for fuel, logging or doing odd chores around the Sechelt Hotel. Before there was a wharf at Sechelt passengers arriving at Trail Bay came ashore from the steamer in small boats. Pete met the hotel guests as they disembarked on the beach and loaded their luggage onto a wooden sledge which was then pulled up the steep incline by a horse.

Pete also owned another primitive little horse-drawn vehicle which he used to transport luggage across the isthmus to Porpoise Bay at a time when the Porpoise Bay Road was little more than a bumpy corduroy trail through a forest of tall trees whose branches sometimes met overhead. The low cart was notable because its two wheels were made from rounds sawn off a fir tree.

tions with the Whitakers was the Carlson family, which during the decade 1904 to 1914 gave its name to no less than three geographic features on the Sechelt Peninsula: Carlson Creek flows from Carlson Lake east into Sechelt Inlet, south of Piper Point, and Carlson Point lies on the west side of Sechelt Inlet across the saltchuck from Gray Creek and Four Mile Point. Members of the family were known by two different surnames, Carlson and Hermanson. The father of the household, Herman Carlson, was born in Sweden about 1845, and in accordance with the ancient Swedish custom his two eldest sons formed their surname from the father's forename and thus were known as Ellis and Ivar Hermanson. The younger sons adopted the new world's form of nomenclature and were known as Eric, Gust and Axel Carlson. The daughters of the house did not become residents of

The Carlson family home up Sechelt Inlet, circa 1912.

One day Pete went into the store to place an order for Cecil Whitaker to deliver. Later in the day Cecil, who operated a boat on Sechelt Inlet, went up to Pete's place at Porpoise Bay to make the delivery and found that Pete had shot himself. He was buried in unconsecrated ground outside the Indian cemetery.

One early family that had firm connec-

Sechelt and apparently lived in the United States.

Ellis and Ivar Hermanson were master carpenters and boatbuilders who worked on a number of projects around the turn of the century for Bert Whitaker. Alfred Whitaker's youngest son, Ronald, described to me the building of his father's beautiful residence, Beach House, later 17 converted into the Sechelt Inn: "The construction work was done by Ellis Hermanson, who was a wonderful carpenter and put up most of Bert's buildings. He later showed me how to build my own cottage." Although there is no proof, it is very likely that Ellis Hermanson constructed Whitaker House, which was completed in the summer of 1907 and for many years stood at the southeast corner of Inlet and Cowrie. He also worked on a barn for the Whitaker family on their farm, which, though now gone, outlasted most of its contemporary buildings, having been used for storage by Union Estates before being sold to serve as a warehouse for Hansen's Transfer. There is no doubt that Ellis Hermanson supervised construction of the tall and graceful Sechelt Indian Church, Our Lady of Lourdes, which was erected in 1906–1907 and destroyed by fire in October 1971. In 1914 Ellis Hermanson volunteered with Thomas John Cook to

Joseph Patrick "Paddy" Hatt at his "Old Egmont" home in 1941, holding one of his famous loaves of whole wheat bread, which he baked in a huge black pan. He purchased wheat by the sack and ground it into flour. The earliest records I have of Paddy are when he registered at the Sechelt Hotel in 1908 and when he donated $2.00 to the Sechelt school building fund in 1914. He earned his living by trapping, fishing, guiding surveyors, prospecting and trail-building. In appearance Paddy was typical of many people of British stock who came to the Sunshine Coast in the early days; they tended to be small in stature, erect in carriage, and magnificent walkers. Their small luxury in life was a pipe of tobacco.

Frank French (left) and his father William James French (1850–1936) on Frank's 40-acre property on the Mason Road, 1919. Frank had just returned from World War One, bringing with him an English bride, Alice Amelia French, well-beloved in Sechelt until her death in 1973. Instead of finding a glamorous estate as her first Canadian home, Alice climbed over logs to this shack in solid bush, lacking even an entrance trail. Old W.J. French came from England to New Westminster, where he operated a butcher shop in the 1880s. About 1910 he retired to live at Sweetpea Ranch in West Porpoise Bay. In 1919 he became a trustee for the Sechelt school.

Abe Mason (seated centre), a logger from Seattle, applied for D.L. 4313 in West Sechelt in 1915. In the early 1920s he moved to the west bank of Cook Creek where it flows into West Porpoise Bay, and built the cottage shown here. His wife Edith (standing in the doorway) had a flower garden which attracted large quantities of beautiful butterflies and she grew delicious strawberries beside the creek. Seated on left is Mrs. Charles Jordan, who lived on the east bank of Cook Creek, with Stan Delong on the right and the Masons' dog Jiggs on the steps. Both Mason and Delong acquired their properties from Thomas John Cook.

build a new public school at the head of Porpoise Bay. The Carlson and Hermanson brothers were still living in Sechelt late in 1914, but prior to the end of the war in 1918 they had all moved to the United States.

WAKEFIELD CREEK PIONEERS

ON DECEMBER 18, 1889, Mr. Joseph Bouillon applied to pre-empt land in West Sechelt at the mouth of a creek which is today known as Wakefield. He paid the crown the sum of $160 and on May 2, 1895 received title to 160 acres described as District Lot 1310, Group 1, NWD.

A Joseph Bouillon was listed as a contractor in Vancouver in 1893, and a Joseph Bouillon came to Sechelt with Father Durieu to work on the Sechelt Indian church Our Lady of the Rosary. Although I have no precise evidence, it seems reasonable to assume that they are the same person.

Throughout the 1890s the creek running through Mr. Joseph Bouillon's land was known as Bouillon's Creek, but this local name was never made official.

By 1902 Mr. W.J. Wakefield was listed in the Sechelt section of the *BC Directory*. Through the ensuing years up to 1923 his occupation was given variously as

farmer, rancher and hand logger. Gradually local people substituted the name Wakefield Creek for the earlier nomenclature.

The West Sechelt area was settled more extensively in the years during and just after the First World War. Families such as the Frenches, Woods, Masons, Delongs and Mitchells were among the pioneers who opened up this part of Sechelt.

OTHER PIONEERS:
Sechelt in 1898

THE 1898 EDITION of *Henderson's British Columbia Gazeteer and Directory* ignored the women of the community completely but named one business and twenty-three men. Of these twenty were described as "farmer," a catch-all word encompassing transients and settlers of divergent backgrounds and occupations. Of the remaining three men, Edward K. Collett was said to be "fisherman and farmer," Mr. Alfred Whitaker was listed as "gentleman," while his son Herbert was "Postmaster" and manager of the "Sechelt Trading Co., general store."

The homes of the twenty-three men were widespread. Frederick Sargeant and Frederick Sargeant Jr. lived at "North 19

West Bay," now more commonly known as Sargeant Bay in their honour.

The area which was later to be named Selma Park was home to a small cluster of settlers in 1898. Edward King Collett lived there and was still in the district during the First World War. A Mr. Finnie lived with his wife and daughter for a short time in the vicinity of Holy Joe's Rock. "Holy Joe" was an authentic eccentric, well known in Vancouver as early as 1890, when he participated in election debates. He acquired his nickname because he belonged to the Salvation Army, but suffered a problem with the drink and had to be re-saved from time to time. Holy Joe moved to District Lot 1329, situated between Sechelt Indian Reserve No. 2 and Davis Bay, where he became so well known that his contemporaries gave his name to the rock bluff above the beach at Selma Park. Another Selma Park resident in the directory is Thomas Harvey, whom I cannot identify.

James Wilson, another man in the 1898 directory, gave his name to Wilson Creek. Although he is described as a "farmer," he was apparently a blacksmith working for the Burns and Jackson logging camp, and may have sold deer to the Sechelt store in 1906. F. Walker and John Walker also made their home in the Wilson Creek area in 1898 and the family continued there for many years, one of them as a boatbuilder.

Thomas Roberts, for whom Roberts Creek is named, had applied to pre-empt District Lot 809 on April 13, 1889 and took his family there in that year to live in a house they built near the shore. They did not remain continuously but Frank Roberts, son of Thomas, returned to the

Totem poles outside the Union Steamship Company pavilion.

Creek with his own sons and daughter in 1900.

Other names mentioned in the 1898 directory are Percy Beken, O.P. Lurn, Joseph Messier, Dan McKenzie, Frank Webster, Daniel White and Charles Young, all of whom were listed as "farmers."

Skeleton Island

THE ARRIVAL OF THE WHITE RACE in British Columbia was detrimental to the welfare of the native people; during late 1862 and 1863 smallpox ran rampant among the BC Indians. This curse almost turned the coast into a vast graveyard. The Catholic missionary Father Fouquet is reported to have vaccinated an estimated 8,000 people while Fathers Chirouse and Durieu together performed the same service for as many more Indians in various regions of the province.

The late Chief Alfie August holding a genuine skull and crossbones during the early summer of 1964.

Today the Sechelt Indians are aware of massive numbers of bones to be found in the area of their homes, because at the time of the plagues there were too few survivors to give attention to the bodies of those who suddenly died. Clarence Joe recalled that his father, Basil Joe, once told him the last smallpox epidemic in Sechelt occured in 1886. During sewage excavation work in 1964 the men doing the digging found everywhere the skeletons of both adults and children.

At the time of the arrival of the Europeans, the Sechelt Nation was scattered along the coast from Stillwater to Howe Sound. They sometimes buried their dead in boxes placed in trees on Poise Island, which until 1945 was known locally as "Skeleton Island," "Dead Man's Island" or "Cook's Island." (In that year the Canadian Hydrographic Service submitted the new name "Poise" and regrettably this became official.) Across the isthmus from this bay was the settlement of what was then called Chatelech. In the past invading tribes from the north had easy access to Chatelech, so the residents were slaughtered by their enemies as well as by disease. Stories have been told of Haida warriors taking youngsters from Chatelech as slaves. Clarence Joe pointed out, however, that the Haida were not responsible for wiping out Chatelech, and that the last raid upon the Sechelt Nation was made at a village on the mainland shore of the Skookum Chuk by the Kwakiutl. The people from the Jervis Inlet then came down their arm of the sea to attack the Nimpkish Kwakiutl in retaliation.

Former chief Alfie August once theorized that some of the bones might be those of Haida Indians who died during tribal fighting. Chief August also recalled that when he was digging out a basement some years ago he found and carefully removed the skeletons of a man, woman and small child. All were in a sitting position. The chief's mother-in-law, Mrs. Paul, explained to him that in earlier times a body was put in a rough wooden box and buried with the dead in a sitting position.

THE OPENING OF SECHELT: SEAWAYS AND ROADS

SEAWAYS:
Boat Landings and Wharves: The Only Access to Early Sechelt

ACCESS TO SECHELT in the early days of its development was almost exclusively by sea. This meant that establishing a landing for sea traffic was instrumental in the community's development. The first such landing was a wharf established at Porpoise Bay by Herbert Whitaker prior to 1904. Joe Gregson, who ran a tugboat called the *Reliance*, owned by Sam Gray as part of his logging operation, remembered the wharf well. It was used at that time by the *Reliance* and by Cecil Whitaker's boat, the *Babine*. Joe described the wharf as a small thing which was sometimes left high and dry when the tide was low. The

name commonly used in the early days to describe the area of Sechelt facing Trail Bay. Having established this access he sought to promote it as a resort as well as a thoroughfare. As proprietor of the "Sechelt Fashionable Seaside Resort" he inserted an advertisement in July 1904 in

The *Babine* on Porpoise Bay sometime between 1908, when it was built for Cecil Whitaker, and 1912, when it burned and sank in Porpoise Bay.

The busy little harbour at the head of Porpoise Bay, circa 1904. The canoe in the lower left corner is a genuine Sechelt Indian style of handcrafted boat, propelled by paddles. The Yamamoto Boat Works building, just left of centre, was where the father and uncle of Clarence Joe had commissioned the building of the first gas boat owned by members of the Sechelt Indian Band, and was later used to house the second Sechelt school. Eventually H.J. Mills, for whom Mills Road is named, dismantled the building to use the lumber for other purposes. The first Porpoise Bay wharf, constructed for Bert Whitaker about 1903, did not jut straight out into the bay but instead ran close along the rock bluff just west of the existing wharf, before short-sighted developers dumped fill which altered the natural character of the shoreline.

Reliance once got stuck in the mud while tied up at the wharf during a falling tide and Joe had to use a Spanish windlass to get her free. He said the old dock was situated about where the present wharf is located.

By 1904 Bert Whitaker had also built a wharf at "the Front," which was the

a Vancouver newspaper, stating that his properties enjoyed "Good roads and wharves, and no mosquitoes or muddy water." As managing director of the Sechelt Steamship Company, Mr. Whitaker ran another advertisement in April 1907, setting out the hours when the steamship *Sechelt* left Vancouver for the 23

Not many people are aware that Sechelt village once simultaneously enjoyed two wharves projecting out from the Boulevard into Trail Bay. One was built in 1904 at the southern terminus of the Porpoise Bay Road. The second pier, pictured here, was erected in front of Beach House adjacent to the southern end of Trail Avenue, which had not been opened up at the time. This wharf, according to the late Ronald Whitaker, was a flimsy thing which did not last long. The two youngsters on the pebble beach were Kenneth Whitaker, 1909–1954, and Isobel Whitaker (later Mrs. W.D. Gilbert), 1910–1976. They were the children of Mae and Herbert Whitaker, who owned both piers. The cottage on the left was one of Whitaker's rental properties.

village of Sechelt, where she connected with the *Newera*. On Tuesdays and Fridays the *Newera* made a trip from the Porpoise Bay wharf to Narrows Arm, while on Mondays and Thursdays she ran to Jervis Inlet. Both boats were owned by Whitaker.

A great portion of the countryside was being logged off at this time and men were constantly on the move across Sechelt Isthmus, a natural centre of activity, and Bert Whitaker took advantage of this. He charged freight for merchandise carried on his steamers, wharfage at both his local docks and cartage when his team transported goods and chattels across the isthmus between the Front and the Bay. T.J. Cook made a note in his journal that all gasoline boats using the float at the Porpoise Bay wharf were charged $2.50 per month, while lockers cost $2.00 per month. In May 1917 Mr. Whitaker is-

212 - PORPOISE BAY WHARF
SECHELT B C

Prior to the present government wharf at the head of Porpoise Bay, built in 1924, there were two wharves in the area. Charles Bradbury, telegraph operator at Sechelt, photographed the float at the end of Whitaker's wharf about 1913 or 1914, showing the style of pleasure craft of the day. The *Resort* (on right) was Bert Whitaker's yacht. Immediately behind the tallest pile in this illustration is a second wharf near the foot of Shoal Way, built by a logger named Parsons. The clearing opposite the end of the float was the Jiro Konishi farm, which was a productive operation between the two world wars.

The government-constructed wharf at Porpoise Bay sometime in the late 1920s or early 1930s. Bryce Fleck's boathouse is on the east side of the wharf. The buildings on the east shore of the bay are likely Indian cabins.

PORPOISE BAY, SECHELT INLET, B.C.

H. McCALL, PHOTO.

sued a receipt to the Union Steamship Company of BC for $25.00 on account of dockage dues for April.

In December 1913 Mr. Whitaker sold his Sechelt properties to a German syndicate, the Canadian-European Investment Company. After war broke out in 1914 the new owners failed to make the installment payments due and Mr. Whitaker had to take legal action to recover his townsite. This is probably the reason the Porpoise Bay wharf was allowed to fall into such a state of disrepair that it collapsed on July 29, 1915.

In 1916 Bert Whitaker renewed the dock and continued to be the proprietor of the Porpoise Bay wharf until midway through the 1920s. He grew ill at that time and his wharf fell into a state of dilapidation again. The people living up

Sechelt Inlet felt strongly the need of a better facility from which they could transport their essential supplies. Mrs. Jessie Irvine, wife of Harry Duncan Irvine, was instrumental in petitioning the federal government to build a wharf at the Bay. She obtained signatures from large Vancouver suppliers such as the Woodward's and David Spencer department stores. The petition succeeded. (Irvine Creek on the east shore of Sechelt Inlet is named for Duncan and Jessie Irvine, who settled in the area in 1912. Their popular creekside home, imaginatively called "Heronsghyll," was accessible only by water for many years. They should not be confused with Charles Irvine, merchant and postmaster, after whom Irvine's Landing is named.)

The government wharf superstructure was renewed in 1969. The floats have been renewed or maintained on an "as required" basis. The seaplane float was installed in 1965. New floats for the wharf were put in place in July 1974, and were built on foam pontoons, which will presumably enjoy a much longer life than fiberglass pontoons or earlier wooden supports.

While the wharf at Porpoise Bay benefited from its renewal in the 1920s, a problem concerning wharfage began to develop in the post–World War Two years with the decline of the Union company—which had taken over Whitaker's estate in the mid 1920s — and the gradual deterioration of the wharf facing Georgia Strait. As early as 1950 James Sinclair,

The original government wharf at Porpoise Bay was constructed in 1923–24. It consisted of a 10-foot by 450-foot approach, 30-foot by 30-foot wharfhead and a 36- by 40-foot float. The location of this wharf was basically the same as that of the present site. Mr. Whitaker's aged wharf remained in its nearby position for some time after the new installation was constructed.

then the local Member of Parliament, declared his support for "increased wharfage and more breakwaters for the Sechelt Peninsula." Then in 1954 the Indian Band presented a brief to the board of trade asking for support to obtain a breakwater between Selma Park and Sechelt. The board set up a breakwater committee in 1960 with Norman Watson as chairman. In the summer of 1960 he

The Selma Park breakwater nearing completion in September, 1967.

Here the *Comox* is seen standing off Trail Bay while she picks up guests from Whitaker's Sechelt Hotel. The luggage was moved up or down the beach in a horse-drawn cart with two home-made wooden wheels. Bert Whitaker stands with his back to the camera holding the reins in his left hand. Rowboats transported passengers and luggage between the tide line and the steamer. Isabel Bell-Irving (later Mrs. S.F.C. Sweeney) remembered one incident involving the wooden vehicle: "I suppose it only happened once but it is still in my memory that the horse took quite a time to get this heavy, horrid thing moving up the beach and when it did go it went with a jerk and all the luggage flew in all directions. I remember we were most tickled with that." At least once, the cart was used as a hearse. The *Comox I* went out of service in 1919 and should not be confused with the motor vessel *Comox II* which operated on Sechelt Inlet in the early 1930s.

and Frode Jorgensen went to Vancouver to drum up support from sailors who had been in distress off the Sunshine Coast. Finally, in 1967, the Federal Works Department awarded the contract for a harbour of refuge at Sechelt to Jim Robb Contracting, and the breakwater was established.

The wharf at Trail Bay was not economically viable even when many ships used the facility, so the Union company was happy to sell it to the federal government in 1933, and a completely new dock was built on the same site. In 1960 the Crown Assets Corporation sold the wharf to the Sechelt Marina and Resort Company. Lack of expensive maintenance resulted in a decaying and hazardous structure, and it was demolished in late 1971.

THE SS *COMOX* AND EARLY TRAFFIC TO SECHELT

VISITORS TO THE SUNSHINE COAST who travel by modern car ferry sail in the wake of a range of historic vessels. The perceptive tourist may see ghosts of ancient Indian dugout canoes or of small sailing ships commanded by such men as the Spanish pilot Jose Maria Narvaez and the British Captain George Vancouver, who in the summers of 1791 and 1792 first mapped the Strait of Georgia. In 1882 Captain Johan Jacobsen, a German ethnologist, blistered his hands on a hot day while paddling down the Strait from Sliammon to the Indian village of Sechelt. Here he met a Chinese merchant travelling in his junk to trade with the native people, and the two men enjoyed a pleasant visit together.

Many years ago there was no wharf at Sechelt, no Cowrie Street, no Highway 101. Access to the city or to the logging camps to the north was by way of the old steamer *Comox*. The *Comox* was wellbeloved along the coast. Early travellers regarded her as having an almost human personality and the popular members of her crew came to know each settler and logger closely. The purser and officers alike did small chores in Vancouver for these isolated people and watched over children journeying alone.

The *Comox* was the first steel vessel assembled in BC, her keel being laid in August 1891 at the Coal Harbour shipyard of her owners, the Union Steamship Company. She measured 101 feet long, 27

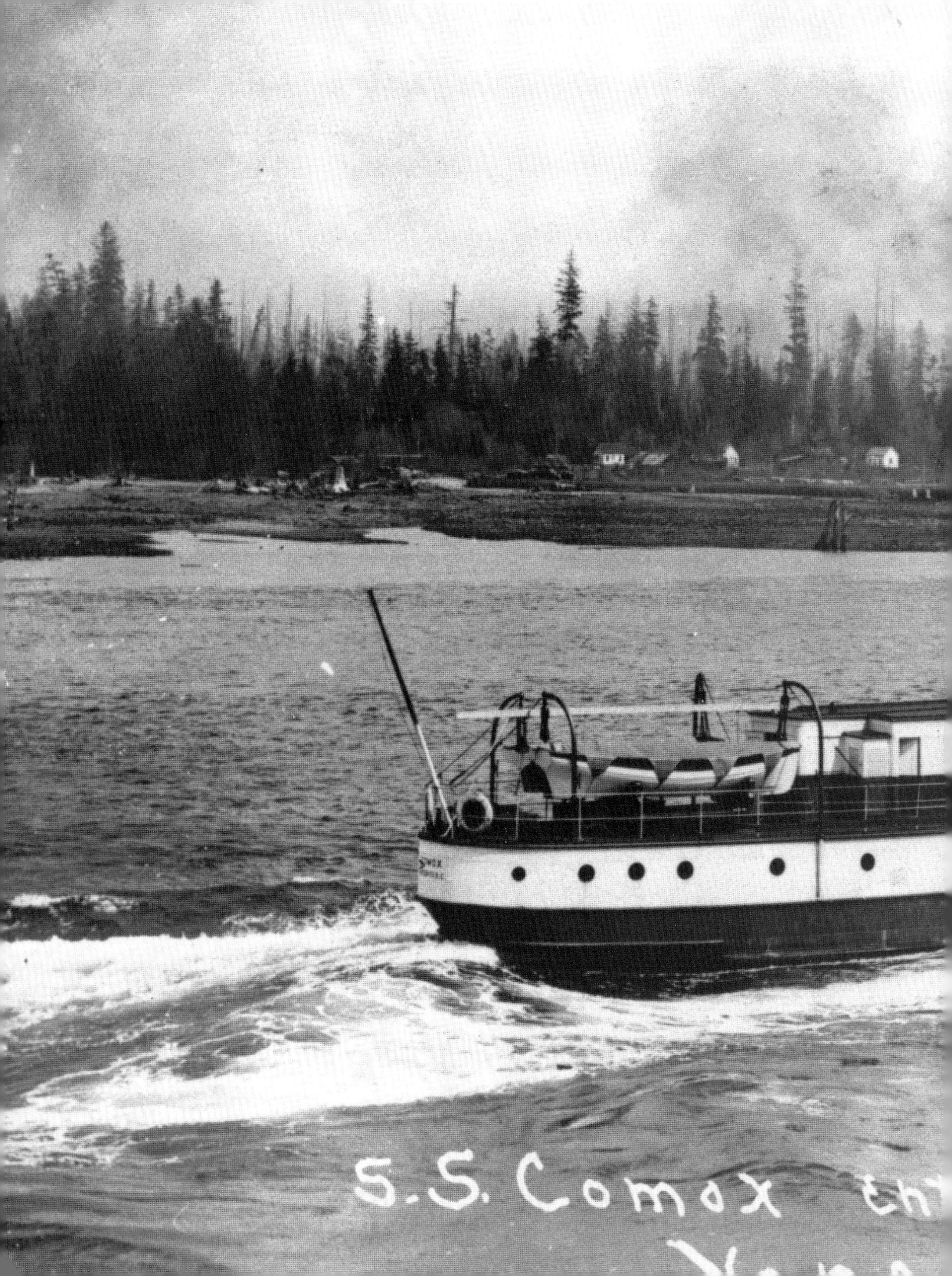
S.S. Comox

The *Comox* entering Vancouver narrows near the turn of the century.

S.CHEKAMUS

The Union Steamship Company's SS *Chekamus* at Sechelt wharf on Trail Bay circa 1913–14. She was built as SS *Cheslakee* in 1910 at the Dublin Dockyard, where nearby the great liners *Titanic* and *Olympic* were under construction. The *Cheslakee* sank alongside the wharf at Vananda in January 1913, resulting in the death of three passengers and the second cook. This was the only accident involving loss of life in a Union passenger ship in the company's history. The *Cheslakee* was raised, lengthened 20 feet, and returned to service in June 1913 under a changed name, *Chekamus*. After long years of service along the Sunshine Coast and northern route, carrying passengers and freight, the ship was converted into a towboat in 1941 and sold to the US government as a salvage tug. The man walking past the damaged area of the Sechelt wharf was Bert Whitaker, who still owned the structure in 1913. The pile driver and donkey engine were kept on the dock to effect repairs after storms. Note the stack of cordwood for fuel.

18 feet across the beam and had a 5-foot depth, which enabled her to function close inshore along the Sunshine Coast before any wharves were built. Her speed of eleven knots was achieved on a coal consumption of 4½ tons in twenty-four hours.

The SS *Comox* operated on a very elastic schedule, according to the amount of cargo and passengers available in town and at various logging camps, mines, ranches and small communities on the shores of Georgia Strait as far up as Port Neville.

Although there was no wharf in Sechelt until about 1904, the *Comox* did not usually put her nose up on the beach to discharge passengers. Rowboats trans-ported passengers and luggage between the tideline and the steamer. Ada Dawe remembered that in 1901, when she was seven years old, her father, Thomas John Cook, brought her for a few days to stay at the Sechelt Hotel. Upon returning to Vancouver they went out from the Trail Bay shore in a rowboat at four o'clock in the morning to board the *Comox*. Percy Chick, the vessel's famous purser, brought a blanket and put it around the child in the cold morning air. Mr. J.P. Chick drowned near First Narrows in 1906 when the *Chehalis* was struck by the *Princess Victoria*.

With the establishment of improved landing facilities for ships there came a number of other Union vessels that took passengers in and out of Sechelt. They include the *Lady Cecilia*, the *Lady Cynthia*, the *Lady Alexandra*, the *Lady Evelyn* and the *Lady Rose*. The SS *Chelhosin*, the *Camosun I*, the SS *Chekamus* and the SS *Melmore* also made runs to Sechelt, as did the paddlewheeler *Yosemite*, a ship that was not in the Union fleet but which made one of the first tourist excursions to the Whitaker hotel as well as earlier charter runs to the Indian settlement.

THE *SECHELT* AND THE *TARTAR*

OTHER SHIPS THAT PLAYED A ROLE in the opening of the Sechelt area were those in Whitaker's Sechelt Steamship Company. The steamer *Sechelt* was one that plied the Sechelt–Vancouver run. It was a small (70–80 feet long, 15-foot beam and 6½-foot hold), narrow, wooden-hulled, shelter-deck, coal-burning steam vessel. She was built as the *Hattie Hansen* at Pontiac for the Lake Washington service in 1893. Subsequently she was used on various other American services, including the Hood Canal mail run and ports on Puget Sound. She was sold to

The large, handsome, speedy and luxurious sidewheel steamer *Yosemite* visited Sechelt several times during the period 1890–1902. Here she is seen in Vancouver Harbour in 1887.

Bert Whitaker in late 1906 or early 1907, renamed *Sechelt*, and became the second vessel of his fleet operated on the Vancouver–Sechelt route. The first ship on the route was the *Newera* and the third was called the *Tartar*.

The *Sechelt* operated mainly on the run between Vancouver and Sechelt, carrying freight and passengers, who paid a $1.00 fare each way. Many way-points such as Bowen Island, Keats Island,

The ill-fated SS *Sechelt* leaving Sechelt wharf with the Trail Islands in the background. She capsized in the Strait of Juan de Fuca in 1911.

Granthams Landing, Gibsons Landing, Cascade Flume and Wilson Creek were also served, and in 1910 the *Sechelt* was placed briefly on trips from Vancouver up Indian Arm to Buntzen and return. Several of these places were boat landings; that is, there were no wharfs and people came out in their boats from Cassadys, Roberts Creek and Wilson Creek to meet the steamers. Keats Island and Granthams Landing each had a float at the time and there were wharves at Hopkins Landing, Gibsons Landing and Sechelt.

Coal for refueling the *Sechelt* and the *Tartar* was stored on the Sechelt wharf, which was also owned by Bert Whitaker. The *Newera* burned wood, and cordwood for her use was kept on a float in front of the Indian Church. It was in Whitaker's Sechelt Hotel that the crews of his vessels took their meals, because there was no provision for the preparation of food on any of these boats. If the men were to be out any length of time they carried a lunch from the hotel, and passengers no doubt followed suit.

While skipper of the *Tartar* in 1912, Captain Sam Dawe received $125 per month plus some meals, and it is pre-

The *Tartar* in Trail Bay between 1909 and 1913.

sumed that wages aboard the *Sechelt* a little earlier would have been similar.

Passengers, mail and freight were carried by the *Sechelt*. When animals such as horses or cows were on her manifest they sometimes had to "walk the plank" and swim ashore. In August 1910 the *Sechelt* struck a reef at the entrance to Vancouver Harbour and in November of the same year she grounded on Bowen Island.

In January 1911 the *Sechelt* was sold to Captain H.B. James, operating as the British Columbia Steamship Company. One source says she was bought by the Sooke Harbour Railroad Company, but this seems to be erroneous. On March 1,

The *Tartar* listing at Lund in 1910.

1911, the *Sechelt* began running between Victoria and Sooke in the Strait of Juan de Fuca—dangerous waters for a small vessel. Just a few days later, on either March 24 or 25, she encountered the storm which resulted in her loss. Captain Stromgren, her regular master, had been relieved by Captain James when she sailed from Victoria, discharged passengers and freight at William Head, passed Beechy Head and then was forced to turn back because of the heavy wind and seas. The *Sechelt* lay over on her port side, but righted temporarily. When the gale hit her again she foundered for a short time and sank. One of the Becher Bay Indians,

to arrive in Vancouver in June 1907. Ownership was transferred to the Sechelt Towage Company, of which Whitaker was managing director. After towing logs for a time, the *Tartar* was converted into a passenger vessel, which made her first trip to Sechelt in May 1909. She was sold to the Sechelt Steamship Company in November and in March 1910 she grounded on a reef near Lund, fell on her side and overturned. The *Tartar* was also salvaged by the ocean tug *William Jolliffe*.

She continued her runs along the Sunshine Coast until Whitaker laid her up in Porpoise Bay during the winter of 1912–13. In 1914 the Vancouver Steamship

The SS *Selma* in Trail Bay, probably between 1913 and 1914, prior to the removal or her aft mast.

Henry Charles, witnessed the catastrophe from the beach and ran to Rocky Point with the news. His message was telephoned to William Head and a launch was sent from there to Victoria. Victoria, in turn, sent out a tug, the *William Jolliffe*, but only a very few bodies were picked up later. The number of men drowned was estimated at between twenty and thirty.

The *Tartar* was built as a tug in Britain and purchased by Herbert Whitaker in 1906, then steamed around Cape Horn

Company (formerly Sechelt Towage Company) sold the *Tartar* to Grant, Smith and Company and McDonnell Limited, who converted the vessel back into a tug. In 1927 title was acquired by E.G.P. Hopkins, of the family for which Hopkins Landing was named, and in 1928 the *Tartar*'s appellation was changed to *Hawser*. Thomas Eustace Hopkins was instantly killed when he fell on the ice-coated deck of the *Hawser*. The ship was dismantled and her certificate canceled in 1938.

A Candle and a Balky Engine
(by Sam Dawe)

THE FOLLOWING STORY was originally told by my father, Captain Sam Dawe, who was at one time skipper of the SS *Tartar*.

In early 1913 I was offered a job as mate on the *Christella*, a boat which had been built to operate on the Howe Sound run. As I had nothing in sight at the time I accepted the job.

There were only four in the crew; the skipper Dave Scoular, a man I knew only as Mr. Brown, Joe Crabtree the engineer, and myself as mate. As near as I can remember she was about 70 feet long, powered with a 100 HP Wolverine engine— the first, last and only one I ever wish to see.

On March 15, 1913 we left Vancouver and made our usual calls at Gambier, Hopkins, Granthams, Keats and Gibsons. At about 4 p.m., on our way back to Vancouver, just off Hood Point on the northern tip of Bowen Island, the engine stopped and in spite of anything the engineer could do it refused to start. There was a slight northerly wind which was setting her on to Hood Point. So we got one of the two 12-foot boats she carried in the water and with Mr. Brown and myself pulling with two pairs of oars and the skipper and engineer keeping her off the rocks with pike poles, we managed eventually to get around the Point and into Grafton Bay, or as it is now called, Cates Bay.

There were several piles there. I don't know what purpose they served but they were a godsend as we were able to tie up to them. After we were tied up, Joe Crabtree started to see what he could do with the engine. I know very little about engines, and internal combustion engines were rather rare in this neighbourhood at that time. I don't think Joe knew too much about them either as he was essentially a steam engineer. There was a base on the engine which opened aft. So Joe got the cover off, with the rest of us watching or trying to help, along with several passengers, though fortunately there were no ladies.

Joe got a candle, lit it, and knelt by the open base of the engine with his face close to it and put the candle inside the base to see what didn't make it tick. Then it happened.

Captain Sam Dawe (right) sitting on the deck of the *Tartar* in 1912. The man on the left is "Little Charlie" Nordin, the mate. The man in the centre is unidentified.

There was a terrific explosion and a blast of fire. It felt as if the whole ship had blown up. When we recovered from the shock there was Joe on the engine room floor, and what a mess he was; his face, arms and hands were badly burnt.

We had nothing on board to treat burns, so we got him up to the cabin and smeared him in engine oil, the only thing we had. We then discussed what was best to do. There was no means of communication that we knew of anywhere nearby. We were not sure if there was a telephone at Snug Cove, which was about 2½ miles away, and there were very few people living anywhere on that part of Howe Sound at that time. So we decided that Brown and I should take the 12-foot boat and start for Vancouver to get help—about 13 miles—and leave Dave Scoular to look after Joe and the ship.

It was about 6:30 p.m. when we

started and at first made good time, but as we got towards Entrance Island a southeasterly wind came up and it started to rain hard, which slowed us some. Eventually we got to Point Atkinson and around it. By this time there was considerable water in the boat and Brown and I were both soaked to the hide, so we pulled into Skunk Cove, where the pilot station used to be, but was now abandoned. There were floats there and we pulled the boat up to one of them to empty the water out of her, after which we put her in the water again and started once more for Vancouver. Luckily there was a flood tide in the First Narrows, which was a great help.

We arrived at Hinds Slip at the foot of Gore Avenue at midnight. Hinds Slip was operated by Jack and Bert Hinds and was frequented by a number of small individually owned and operated tug boats. On the way in we had agreed that Brown would see about getting an ambulance and I would see about getting a tug to bring the *Christella* in. When we got ashore Brown started for home to get out of his wet clothes.

The first thing I did was go to the office on the wharf. There was no one there but the door was not locked so I went in and telephoned my parents, who lived on W. 8th Avenue, and told them not to expect me for a while, after which I started to look for a tug. There were several at the slip but all were in darkness except one, the *Clara Young*, a small steam tug which was showing a light, so I went on board.

The engineer was there and he was a young French-Canadian whose first name was Steve. I knew him well and explained to him what had happened and what I wanted. He knew Joe Crabtree and was very willing to help, but did not like the idea of going without the consent of the man who owned the tug—a Captain Butler. Steve did not know where to get in touch with the owner, and after telephoning at the office he could still not be located.

I eventually talked Steve into going with the understanding that he would run the engine and I would do the rest. It took him about half an hour to get up steam and at about 2 a.m. we were ready to leave. Brown showed up about then, and we figured as closely as we could when we should get back so Brown could have the ambulance there.

We then left, and it took about two hours to get to the *Christella*. Joe was suffering a great deal of pain but there was not much we could do with him. We hooked on the *Christella* and started for town, arriving at Hinds Slip about 7:30 a.m. The ambulance was there and we got Joe up the slip to the wharf and away he went to the hospital.

I got away for home about 8:30 a.m., and as my sister was being confirmed that morning I had a bath and shave, changed my clothes, and went with my family to the confirmation. After lunch I went to bed and stayed there till the next morning.

Joe Crabtree was in the hospital for a long time. I saw him after he came out and he did not look too bad. The doctors had done a good job on him. The *Christella* was taken to Coal Harbour. I never saw her again as I went away on another job soon after. I heard she had been burnt—how badly I don't know, but I don't believe she ever went back on the Howe Sound run.

So ends the story of the *Christella* and the commandeering of the *Clara Young*. I saw Captain Butler later and he was very kind about the matter and did not blame either Steve or myself for taking his boat that night.

SAILING INTO SELMA PARK

LIKE THE TRAIL BAY AREA, Selma Park was opened up by sea, particularly after 1914, when the All Red Line acquired seven acres of property just east of Sechelt Indian Reserve No. 2 and established a summer resort there. Old Post Office records show that in December 1914 Mr. R. Dunn, game warden, received mail at the address "Selma Park, Sechelt," which is the earliest record I can find of the use of the new place name. Reg Dunn operated the first small store there, shelving the stock in his home.

In 1916 the All Red Line built the first wharf at Selma Park, basing it on Holy Joe's Rock. One of the All Red Line's ships that sailed regularly into the area was the passenger steamer *Selma*, which is where the community got its name. The vessel had been built in Scotland in 1881 under the name *Santa Cecilia*, as a steam yacht for the Marquis of Anglesey. Before coming to BC she had had several other owners.

In 1910 Captain Polkinghorne of Vancouver purchased the ship and commanded her on a voyage of 15,500 miles, leaving Plymouth in August and arriving

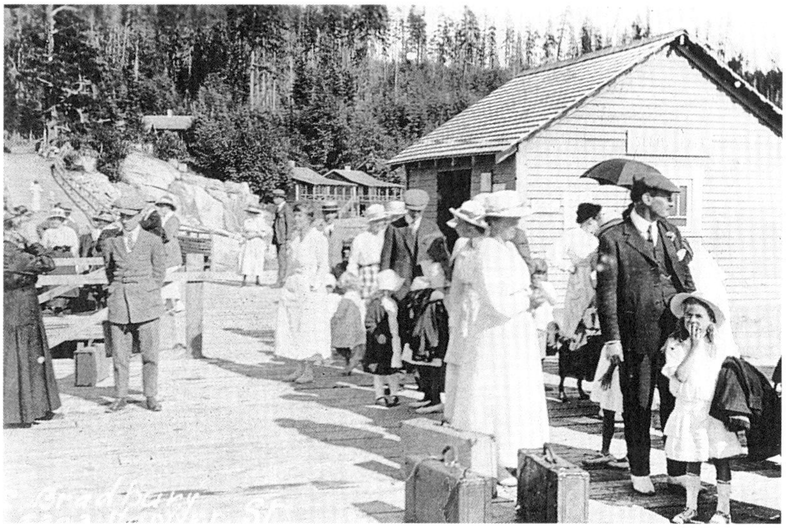

Passengers waiting to sail from the Selma Park wharf in 1920. Behind them is Holy Joe's Rock.

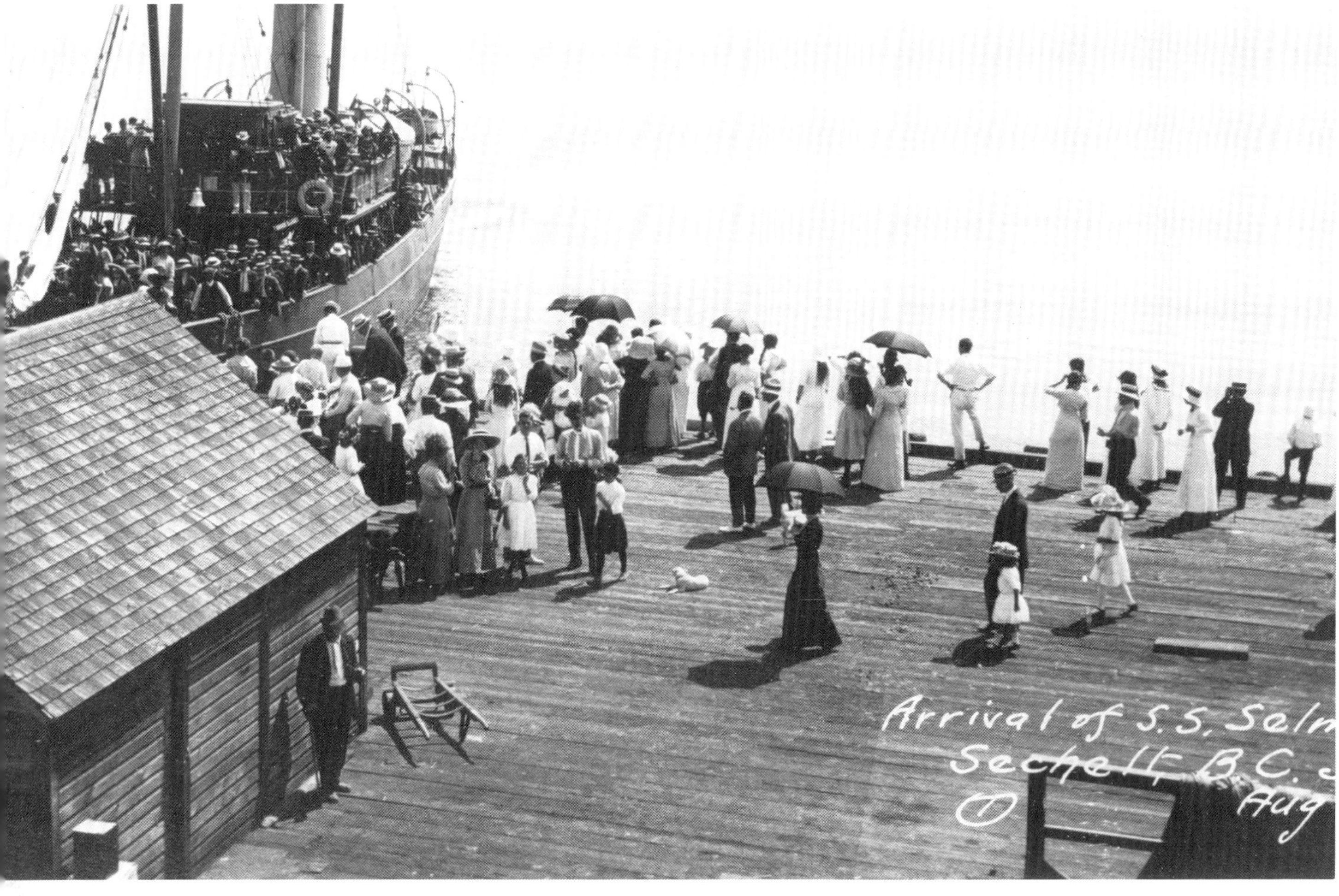
Arrival of S.S. Sel
Sechelt, B.C.
Aug

The SS *Selma* arriving at the Sechelt wharf in August of 1913.

The SS *Chilco* docking at the Selma Park wharf with the Sechelt waterfront in the background.

in Vancouver in December 1910 by way of the Straits of Magellan. Polkinghorne was a principal in the All Red Line (incorporated in January 1911), which ran the steamships *Selma* and the 154-foot *Santa Maria*—purchased by the company in 1914—between Vancouver and Powell River, with stops at various wharves and floats along the Sunshine Coast. Stanley Mills, who came to live in West Sechelt in 1915, remembers that in his boyhood the two steamers passed each other in front of his father's house, one headed upcoast and the other headed to Sechelt wharf.

Then in 1917 the All Red Line sold its

ships, together with its land and wharf at Selma Park, to the Union Steamship Company. The Union company renamed the *Selma* the *Chasina*, and she continued to serve the Sunshine Coast until she was sold in 1923 to become a rum runner. When the liquor trade slumped the old vessel was sold yet again and she sailed for Macao, a port involved in the drug trade. The *Chasina* cleared from Macao for Vancouver but was never heard from again. The *Santa Maria* became the *Chilco* in 1917 and *Lady Pam* in 1935. After the war the old vessel was sunk as a breakwater at Oyster Bay.

Sechelt and the First World War

IN THE SUMMER OF 1914 the local population was agog with a story that the Germans intended to take over Sechelt for use as a hospital base. Ronald Whitaker recalled that when he lived at Selma Park, the local priest, Father Wagner, came to tea and his topic of the day was the Germans' plan to make Trail Bay their headquarters.

In 1914 the coastal area of BC was full

of tales of German espionage, and German naval vessels were thought to be in the vicinity, ready for attack. Dr. Margaret Ormsby, in her book *British Columbia: A History*, says that "during the last days of July and the first days of August, an absolute certainty prevailed in government circles that Admiral von Spee and his China squadron intended to bombard and capture Vancouver and Victoria and then, in co-operation with German residents, establish a foothold on the Pacific

Coast."Richard McBride, premier of BC at that time, sent an agent to Seattle in August 1914 arrange for the purchase of two submarines recently completed there for the government of Chile. The submarines were delivered and paid for by a Province of BC cheque in the amount of $1,150,000. Our provincial navy lasted for three days until the federal government took over the submarines on August 7 for use by the admiralty. Constantin Alvo von Alvensleben, a German resident of Vancouver, was one of the chief sources of suspicion in local rumours of espionage. He had married a British Columbia girl, Edith Mary Westcott, and she was the friend of a sister of Bert Whitaker. In 1913, through the agency of von Alvensleben, who was in the real estate business, Mr. Whitaker sold his Sechelt properties to Baron von Lutwitz, another German. The holdings included the Sechelt Hotel, the general store and several rental cottages, all of which were thought to figure in German military plans for hospital accommodation. Ada Dawe recalled that after the outbreak of war in 1914, rumour circulated that the customs department in Vancouver had seized parcels containing hospital medical supplies consigned to Sechelt, and that the hotel clerk at Sechelt had an uncle who was an admiral in the German navy. The clerk fled to Seattle and was later removed from a vessel at Gibraltar and interned by the British.

The first time Baron von Lutwitz visited Sechelt just prior to the war he stayed with Thomas P. O'Kelly, a partner of Bert Whitaker. One day Mr. O'Kelly and Baron von Lutwitz went off on a fishing expedition, from which the Baron returned with a small sack of mud. He said he was taking the sample away to have it tested for possible use in making bricks. Of course when war broke out his motive was questioned. He also had a gun with a telescope, the first such combination seen in these parts, and he was often observed viewing the area through the telescope. Such incidents had the suspi-

Gustav Constantin Alvo von Alvensleben.

cious bristling with interest.

Alvo von Alvensleben crossed the border and was interned at Salt Lake City when the United States entered the war in 1917. In 1965 he died in Seattle at the age of 86.

As a footnote there is an interesting chronicle about von Alvensleben to be read in Cicely Lyons' book *Salmon: Our Heritage*. She tells in detail how von Alvensleben and Associates erected a cold storage, reduction and ice plant in 1910 on Selwyn Inlet, off Hecate Strait. The property was purchased by BC Packers in 1938, when the old building was demolished. An underground concrete installation was then discovered and was examined by experts. They formed the opinion that it was "evidently planned for use as a submarine base."

ROADS

MANY OF THE EARLIEST ROADS in the Sunshine Coast were skid roads and trails constructed by loggers or miners. Noel Humphreys, a surveyor, was working on the mainland side of Sechelt Inlet in 1924. His report includes the following comment on local mining roads half a century previously: "It is remarkable the work which was accomplished by the old mining company around the year 1876. They constructed a first-rate horse trail from Salmon Arm to the meadows on Slippery Creek to an elevation of 3,100 feet. From there they apparently packed everything right up the canyon the same way I ran my traverse."

Closer to Sechelt, the Porpoise Bay Road was built in 1896 to facilitate the transfer of freight between Trail Bay and the head of Sechelt Inlet. The provincial government expended $87.50 in the construction of the road, incorporating a portion of the ancient Indian trail between the two waterways. Bert Whitaker was in charge but the actual building of

The road leading into the Sechelt Indian lands circa 1900–1906, with Our Lady of the Rosary Church in the background.

the road was done by T.J. Cook and two members of the Sechelt Band. They dragged boom chains over the road to level it. The road was blacktopped in 1956, around which time the initial three or four blocks became known as Wharf Avenue.

Part of this road originally went across what is now known as the Sechelt Marsh, and at high tide the water would come up and cover it. Arnold McQuarrie, who as a teenager worked for Bert Whitaker be-

A dusty wagon road now named Wharf Avenue (ex Porpoise Bay Road), photographed in 1904 by Philip Timms. The fence enclosed Bert Whitaker's farm on the left adjoining the reserve. The water tower on the right stood roughly where the northwest corner of Cowrie Street and Wharf Avenue is today.

tween 1917 and 1919, recalled an occasion when he was sent to Porpoise Bay from Trail Bay to pick up a passenger who had just come down the inlet with her baggage. Arnold drove the horse-team while standing on a flat-decked wagon. The tide had come in over the road in the area of the marsh and the heavy lady passenger, who was sitting on the wagon deck, got her nether parts wet. She complained bitterly to Arnold's employer, but the boy himself had been so busy guiding the team that he had not noticed the water at his feet. A foot-bridge, 375 feet long, was built across the marsh in 1913 for $166.95, though by 1920 the bridge had become quite dilapidated.

Porpoise Bay on its easterly side was analyzed in the report of the Minister of Lands for 1916. One area which had been divided into twelve claims, opened for pre-emption, was described by the surveyor: "In logging, oxen or horses were used for draught purposes, and the roads then made, though somewhat grown up, could readily be improved to give access to these lands. In shingle-bolting, some of the old roads have been opened up and connected to a landing and chute on the east side of the Bay in Lot 4688."

The footbridge across Porpoise Bay Marsh (often referred to as the "Bog," the "Swamp" or "Lagoon") circa 1915.

Government Road (now Sunshine Coast Highway) through Selma Park in 1915. Ken Walton, the child on the left, wrote that "the picture is of my grandfather, Edwin F. Walton, and me, packing water between the well (which was near the old tennis courts) and Uncle George's house." Members of the Walton family, who summered at Selma Park for many years, were associated with Johnson, Walton Steamships Ltd. as well as the All Red Line. Note the telegraph poles and lines along the inshore side of the road.

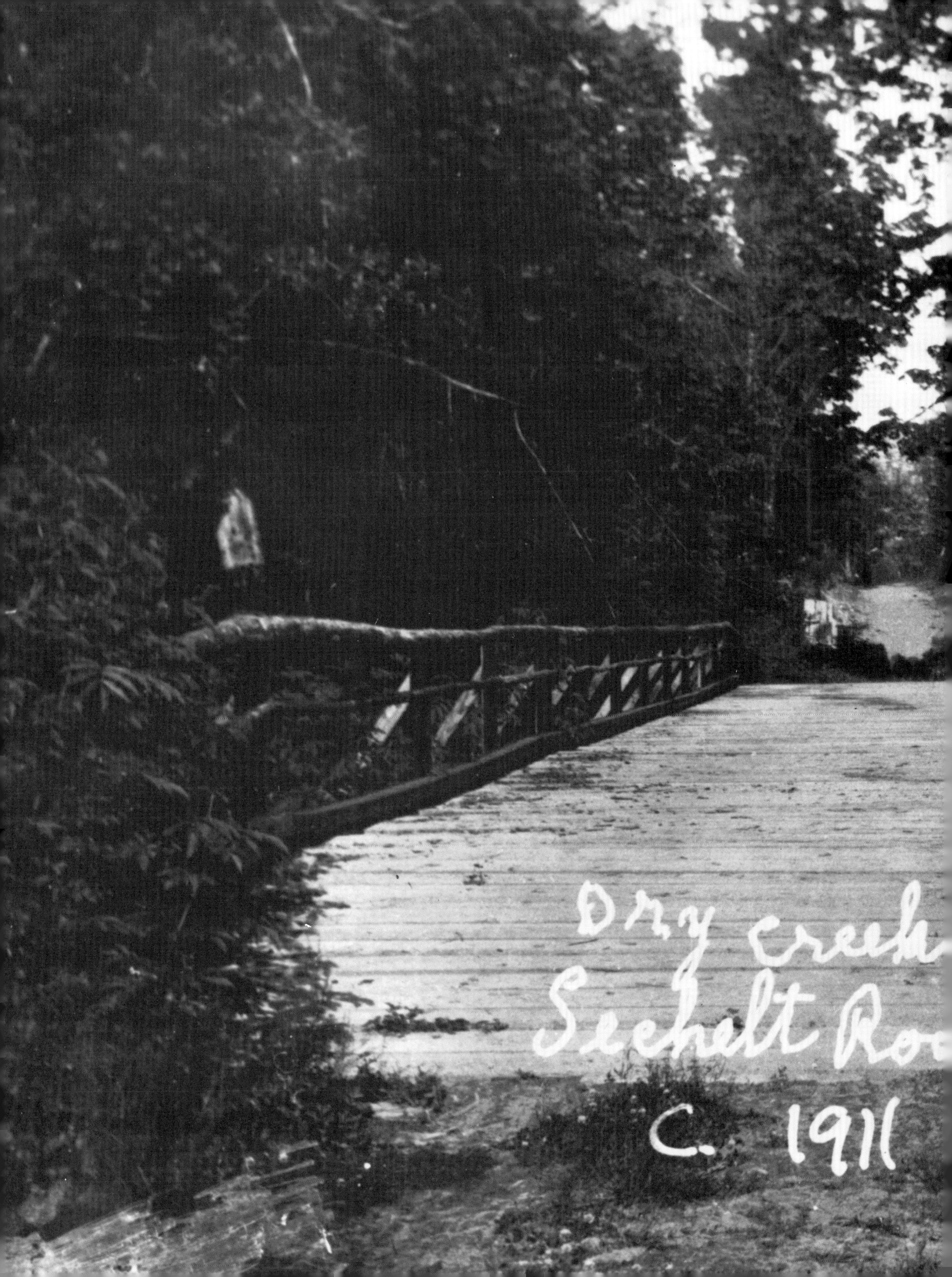
Dry creek
Sechelt Ro
C. 1911

A bridge over one of the creeks crossing the road to Sechelt in 1911.

Many of the streets in Sechelt were given their names by Bert Whitaker in civic plans that were drawn up in 1909. Dolphin Street, Medusa Street and Ocean and Trail Avenues were among the streets named by Whitaker, as were Barnacle, Teredo, Cowrie, Inlet, Marine and many others.

In 1911 a primitive wagon route was opened between Sechelt and Selma Park, making it possible to drive a cart overland to Gibsons, but there was still no bridge over Chapman Creek, which had to be forded. Highway 101 was initially known as the Sechelt Highway or Upper Sechelt Road. Even as automobile use increased in subsequent decades, this road and others remained poor. In 1944 the *Coast News* reported that "conditions of Peninsula roads have become so serious that residents are organizing volunteer crews to make repairs. Trucks and cars in Sechelt are forced to dodge mud holes in the roads by using boulevards and foot paths along a quarter mile stretch through the village, thus forcing pedestrians to walk on the road." In 1947 the same paper reported that "rural mail service in this district has been suspended due to impassable roads." And by 1948

the problem had become so serious that even the *Vancouver Daily Province* took note of it:

Part of an old railway logging line, possibly up Sechelt Inlet.

Sechelt District Board of Trade members are so mad about their main road they are going out Sunday to work on it themselves.

Dump trucks have been donated, white collar lads will climb behind the steering wheels, volunteers will man shovels. They are going to fill potholes over a stretch at Wilson

Mr. Todd, road engineer with the BC Department of Public Works, 1918, photographed by Gladys Tidy outside the Sechelt School. Mr. Todd came to the Sunshine Coast once a month for a two-day stay and boarded with the A.S. McCall family in Gibsons. Note the leather gauntlets and horn beside the rider's left hand.

Creek, divert water cascading over the road, and generally do their best to show the Public Works Department they've had enough... The road is so potholed particularly between Gibsons and Sechelt that cars hold down to 15 or 20 miles an hour and go slower where the streams cross the road.

In one two-hundred-foot stretch of road over 390 potholes had been counted. By December 1948 the Public Works Department had got the message

northward, in preparation for the commencement of the government telegraph service in 1913. Prior to the First World War there was no road from the centre of the Sechelt village to Wakefield. Soon the isolation diminished and the BC Public Works Report for the year April 1916 to March 1917 reported that a bridge fifty feet by fourteen feet had been installed over Wakefield Creek.

The Sargeant Bay area at this period was described in the report of the inspector of pre-emptions, who wrote: "The pre-emptions at North West Bay are

Cowrie Street viewed approximately from its juncture with Shorncliffe Avenue between 1936 and 1938.

and gravel trucks were dispatched to repair part of the road between Wilson Creek and Sechelt. The highway was paved in 1952.

In the first decade of the century there was no road at all west of Trail Avenue, but in 1912 work began on the "Telegraph Trail" (later known as Marine Drive) to Pender Harbour, along which wires were strung to Halfmoon Bay and

mostly taken up by loggers who are working in the logging camps in the vicinity, who have built themselves good homes on their land." Some of the roads in this area were forged by settlers seeking to link their property with more central areas. Abe Mason, for instance, built what is now known as Mason Road in order to deliver timber from his property into Trail Bay, probably just after moving 45

A view of the early Sechelt waterfront.

to the area in 1915. By 1920 the only approach to Mason Road was Norwest Bay Road. The first road between Halfmoon Bay and Sechelt was built in 1928, though Redrooffs Road, connecting Redrooffs with Halfmoon Bay, was established back in 1909.

The northerly portion of the peninsula was described in the 1913 report of the Minister of Lands:

> Pender Harbour is well served by the Union Steamship Company and the All Red Line, and boats are coming and going almost daily. The principal lakes on this part of the Peninsula are Killarney, at the north end, Ruby, Sakinaw, and Garden Bay; the three former are separated by portages of less than a mile. Lake Killarney is about two miles by trail from Linden's Camp; it would, however, be quite feasible to replace this by a wagon-road. There are also fairly good trails connecting Killarney and Ruby Lakes, and from the latter to Sakinaw; access is also had to Ruby Lake direct from Agamemnon Channel by means of logging-roads.

By 1929 a road had been forged to Irvines Landing. Some of the road construction done in the upper part of the peninsula in the 1930s was done by men working in Depression-era relief camps. In 1957 the *Coast News* reported that "the last stretch of highway linking Gibsons, Sechelt and Pender Harbour to Powell River has been completed."

Some of the impetus for the construction of a suitable highway running the length of the coast stemmed from the increase in the volume of automobile traffic resulting from the creation of a ferry link between Horseshoe Bay and Gibsons by the Black Ball company in 1951. The Sunshine Coast landing was moved to Langdale in 1959, and Black Ball Ferries was purchased by the BC government in 1961.

It was not until the 1920s that automobiles appeared in Sechelt. The Union Steamship Company had a truck, which may have been owned previously by Bert Whitaker. Between 1928 and 1930 Frank French acquired a car which he used as a taxi, while Joe Martin had a truck which he used as a "bus" as well as for hauling. And Jack Mayne had a Model A Ford.

The Worst Storm in Sunshine Coast History

PIONEERS AT THE EARLY SETTLEMENTS along the coast have published stories or have told younger generations about the famous great gale of Saturday, January 29, 1921, when heavy timber along the coast went down before a southeast wind, creating a shambles in such places as Lang Bay, Egmont and Sechelt.

The wharf at Trail Bay on January 30, 1921, after being ravaged by the worst storm in Sunshine Coast history.

Lang Bay lies on the east side of Malaspina Strait, south of Powell River. *In Great Waters*, a book written by the Reverend George Pringle, includes an account of the storm. He and five others from a shinglebolt camp were walking the mile through the woods to Smith's store at Lang Bay settlement when the 1921 gale "tore down upon us in howling fury. There was no place for shelter from the great branches and limbs that whizzed past us in the darkness, and the giant trees that fell crashing down in all directions around us. The noise of the storm was so great that to make ouselves heard we had to shout into one another's ears."

The marine missionary wrote that he spent the most terrifying hour of his life on that walk, but upon arriving at a house at Smith's clearing he decided to hold his service anyway: "We were nicely started when the window blew in! I caught it on my back, but the lamp was extinguished and the table blown over. It took fifteen minutes to get the window nailed back and everything in order again. I got along to the sermon and was somewhere in 'secondly' when a wild blast commenced to tear the paper off the wall opposite me, against which the people were sitting. It was building paper loosely tacked on in strips from ceiling to floor. Another gust and down it all came, completely covering up my congregation. After they had crawled out it took half an hour before we got that paper tacked up again. Then we closed with the hymn 'For Those in Peril on the Sea.' Millions of feet of standing timber were blown down that night at Lang Bay."Mr. and Mrs. William Griffith and their youngsters settled in August 1920 at a bay east of Egmont Point, which is northeast of Skookumchuk Narrows. They lived in a log cabin which had been built by a relative in 1914. When Mrs. Griffith proposed putting the children to bed on that Saturday evening in January, 1921, Mr. Griffith suggested a delay because a southeast wind was refreshing. Gladys McNutt recorded their story as told to her by Bill, a son of the family. "The Griffiths wrapped up the children and took them out to a bare rocky islet within the bay and spread canvas over them as protection from the flying twigs and needles." Early Sunday morning a few of the men who lived in the Egmont area rowed over to check on the Griffith household. "They breathed a sigh of relief to see smoke coming from the chimney but a huge limb was through the roof immediately above the spot where Mr. Griffith usually sat. They all got busy and felled the maples and alders about the place. Most of the standing timber in the draw had come down."

Florence E. Montgomery and Alice French spoke to me of the gale as it had affected them half a century before. Mrs. Montgomery was at that time Florence Cliff, the first teacher at the original West

Sechelt school. She boarded for a time with Katie Deal and her husband Fred near the Trail Bay beach.

On the Saturday afternoon of the big storm Florence took a bath and dressed in her best for a dance at the Selma Park Pavilion. She was all ready when Mr. Deal arrived home. He told the ladies to put out the lamps and douse the fire to avoid trouble should a tree fall on the house. Then he shepherded his wife, Florence, as well as a neighbour, Mrs. Nickson and her children Rena and Harold, to take shelter on the beach in the lee of a large scow stranded there two or three years earlier.

About one o'clock Sunday morning the wind had abated sufficiently that Fred Deal felt it safe for his charges to return home. A tree had fallen near the Deal house, but both residences in Nickson's Bay were safe. When daylight came they walked up Norwest Bay Road to West Sechelt school and counted twenty-four trees down en route.

Alice French came to Sechelt in 1919 as the English war bride of Frank French. She was a friend of Thomas John Cook who, as resident magistrate, knew everybody for miles about and organized his neighbours to go check on the more isolated homesteads on the day after the storm. He assigned Alice to visit Mr. and Mrs. McIntyre in West Sechelt. She found them flourishing and their home intact, but their outdoor privy had vanished completely.

During the next summer Alice attended a tea party in the McIntyre's garden. She happened to look up into a tree shading her chair and to her amusement saw the can from the lost outhouse perched high on a limb.

It is said that the giant trees and snags which fell before the southeaster usually lay pointing to the northwest, sometimes piled two or three deep. Over the years they provided firewood for the homesteaders. What a vast amount of time and energy it must have cost to get the trunks sawn through before power saws were in use, to clear the primitive roads and to restore downed telegraph wires. Electric lighting did not then exist except for households using private systems. The Sechelt school in 1921 had only candles and the Sechelt store used hanging gas lamps, which gave a nice white light.

H. Victor Whittall travelled to Sechelt by floatplane in 1936, when such a mode of transportation was unusual locally. The aircraft landed on Trail Bay close to the foot of Shorncliffe Avenue, beside the raft of the Bryce Fleck family. Mr. Whittall's destination, Rockledge, was built in 1931 as a summer home for Professor Donald English, a BC man who taught at Cornell University. Mary and Victor Whittall resided in Pink Cottage (later known as Whitaker House) in Sechelt for a time when he was superintendent of the Blue Band Navigation Company's shingle enterprise.

Roy Brett pictured with his aircraft, which at 8:10 a.m., October 1, 1957 became the first plane to land at the Gibsons-Sechelt Municipal Airport.

AIR TRAVEL

AN ARTICLE IN THE *VANCOUVER PROVINCE* of June 12, 1948 said "Porpoise Bay... is an ideal spot for a seaplane landing base because of its calm and sheltered waters. Here the Associated Air Taxi of Sea Island is planning a float so that it can provide a regular charter service." In 1961 Al Campbell started Tyee Airways, which in 1966 was given Transport Board approval to operate a Jervis Bay service out of Sechelt.

Roy Brett, a Selma Park contractor, was the first to land at the Gibsons-Sechelt Municipal Airport in October of 1957, when the airstrip was merely a clearing in the woods. Mr. Brett was awarded a contract for $28,725 for work on the airport, which was originally under the control of the Aero Club. (Roy Brett later went missing without a trace when his plane was caught in a storm on the way from Powell River to Chilliwack in 1982). The airport, located on Field Road near Wilson Creek, was officially opened on May 9, 1962, by then Lieutenant Governor G.R. Pearkes, though the runway was not paved until late 1975. The ramp had to wait until early 1976 to be blacktopped. The airport is presently owned jointly by the villages. Airspan Helicopters opened at the airport in October of 1982.

An early Tyee Airways floatplane hangar in October of 1966, moved to Porpoise Bay from Campbell River where it served Island Airlines.

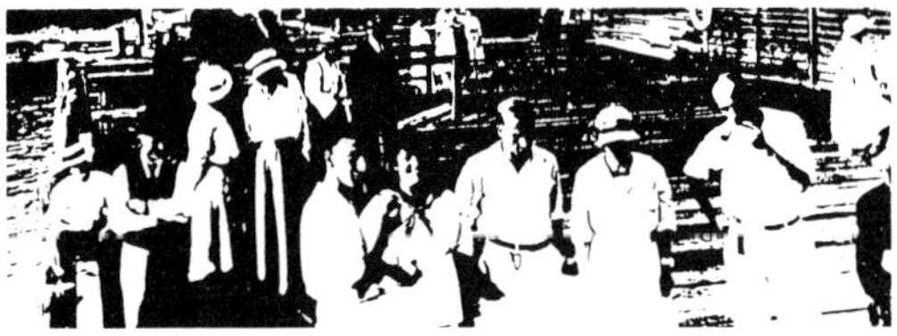

RESOURCES

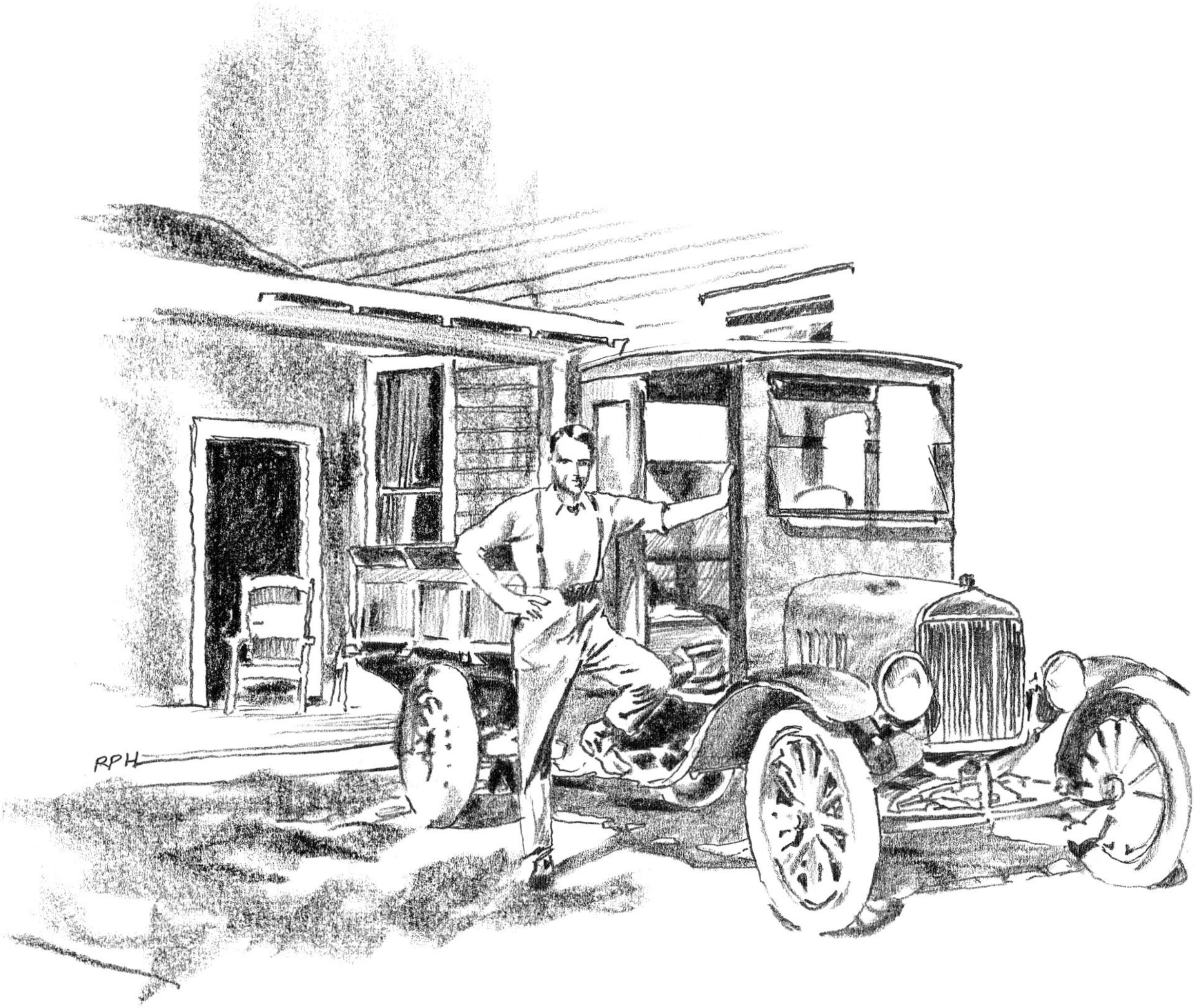
RPH

LOGGING

LOGGING WAS CONDUCTED in the areas around Sechelt from an early date, with many camps in operation up Sechelt Inlet and along Georgia Strait. The first decades of the century saw the Barr and Fraser Company logging at Selma Park, Jackson Brothers at Wilson Creek and the Heaps Company up Sechelt Inlet and Narrows Arm. Before too long more sophisticated machinery was being used, and areas that had been previously inaccessible were being logged over by bigger operations. The Steinbrunners had a logging camp near Roberts Creek in the 1920s that featured a flume, which Betty Ingram (née Youngson) remembered riding down on a shinglebolt "as if it was a sea horse." Much of the mountainside above Roberts Creek was logged by Pete Berdahl in the 1930s, who was using one of the first caterpillar tractors. The B & K Company conducted logging operations in Roberts Creek in the late 1930s and early 1940s,

and Burns and Jackson expanded into the Wilson Creek area about the same time and built a sawmill at the mouth of Wilson Creek. Logging companies located in the Halfmoon Bay area from the 1920s on included the Neimi, Osborne and Rotter companies. Ted Osborne took over Oscar Neimi's operation in 1936.

A 1916 surveyor's report for the Minister of Lands referred to logging in the area east of Porpoise Bay: "As a timber license this land was logged over some considerable time ago, and more recently has been worked over for shingle-bolts." The same report noted that "a small sawmill is in operation, supplying local demand," at the head of Porpoise Bay. This sawmill belonged to Bert Whitaker, who also had a mill at Skookum Chuk in addition to five logging camps up Sechelt Inlet.

Pharic Honeyman, who spent some summers with his family as a boy in early Sechelt, recalled, "In those days [about 1907] they were logging over behind Selma Park. The logs were brought by

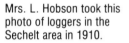
Mrs. L. Hobson took this photo of loggers in the Sechelt area in 1910.

donkey engine to the edge of the cliff and shot down a chute into the booming area. It was always a spectacular sight as the logs hit the water." This was likely the Fraser River Lumber Company. After hitting the water the logs were gathered into booms and towed away by tugs.

Of course there were always a number of accidents associated with logging. Betty Ingram, who in the late 1930s was working as a clerk in the Provincial Police office, remembered that "logging accidents were more prevalent and it always brought me to sadness to go on stenographer duty at an inquest as so very often it

would be a personal friend who had met with misfortune. Everyone knew everyone in those days. Inquests and preliminary hearings were usually held in the old waterfront tea room."

McNair's Shinglebolt Camp

AN EXAMPLE of an early logging operation is McNair's shinglebolt camp at Roberts Creek. Roy Fleming brought his parents, wife and two daughters, Myheera and Phyllis, to live at Roberts Creek around 1924. From then until about 1928 he operated three different

This photo, circa 1913–1914, shows Bert Whitaker's mill at the head of Porpoise Bay. The mill was in operation from as early as 1910.

Myheera Fleming (right) at her father's shinglebolt camp in the 1920s with the foreman "Gurney" and a Japanese child.

The dam at McNair's camp. It held water diverted from local streams until enough shinglebolts were assembled to make a full shipment, at which point the water would be released to carry the shinglebolts down a flume to tidewater.

The flume at McNair's shinglebolt camp at Roberts Creek in the 1920s. It stretched four miles down to the ocean, where barges and tugs would be waiting to carry off the shinglebolts. The flume was equipped with a catwalk along the side to allow workers to free blockages, and telephones at either end provided efficient communication.

shinglebolt camps in the area. The largest camp was high up the mountain, where the west fork of the creek was dammed and feeder dams added to create a pond. Roy Fleming used mules exclusively in taking out the cedar. These animals worked in teams, pulling loads of bolts from the cutting site along primitive skid roads to the creek. Although Mr. Fleming owned the operation himself, he sold his clear cedar longbolts under contract to the Robert McNair Shingle Company, so the camp was commonly known as McNair's.

Within the camp clearing there was a big cookhouse and a huge blacksmith shop, where some of the men lived. Myheera remembered that the boss of the

other workers, a man they called "Gurney," refused to live in the bunkhouse and had a place of his own. Mr. Fleming employed Japanese crews who brought their wives and children with them and lived in their own quarters. Myheera took baths with the Japanese children. Their mothers prepared a large

Logging at Davis Bay in 1923. Left to right: Dave McNutt; Fred McNutt; the owner of the operation; Hector McCall.

wooden bathtub on a platform which was protected by sheet metal from the hot stones placed underneath. Water from the creek flowed into the wooden tub through spouts made from hollowed-out tree branches. Heat from the stones warmed the water.

Matt LeClaire was the flume tender and consequently lived at the mouth of Roberts Creek, on its east bank, with his wife and several children. The flume ran about four miles from the Fleming camp down the mountain through the Reeves' property on Lockyer Hill and out over Harry Roberts' sawmill at the beach. There was telephone communication between the upper and lower ends of the flume.

The dam near the camp was not ordinarily in use, but once sufficient bolts were assembled to warrant a shipment the dam was readied by placing certain boards in position to hold the water until required. A crib was then ordered from the Vancouver area and towed into position at the mouth of Roberts Creek.

Two mules pulling cedar bolts to a dam high up on a mountain behind Roberts Creek at the McNair camp.

In due course the dam was opened enough to create an extra flow of water which would carry the bolts down the flume directly into the crib. Farther down, the flow of water could be controlled to send the shinglebolts into either side of the crib. On one occasion, Mr. Fleming happened to be in Vancouver when a tug arrived to tow away the crib, which was not yet loaded. Myheera and her mother dealt with the emergency by taking pike poles and fluming sufficient bolts down to the beach to provide the tug with a tow. Delivery was made to McNair's mill at Port Moody.

Alongside the flume was a catwalk, one plank wide, upon which the men could walk all the way up the mountain in order to clear any bolts which became stuck. From her youth Sheila Danroth recalled water dripping down through the flume onto passersby when they walked across the Roberts Creek bridge in the vicinity of the store. She was Sheila Reeves at the time and little guessed that when she grew up and married, her hus-

band would use lumber from the old camp buildings to construct a house.

FARMING

A NUMBER OF EARLY SETTLERS had farm plots for growing their own produce. Duncan and Jessie Irvine had an acre of lucrative garden on their property on Sechelt Inlet, and the Carlson family owned 176 acres — three of which were under cultivation — and several barns for livestock. Though he was primarily a logger, Abe Mason kept chickens and pigs with his logging horses in a field behind his house. Jack Wood, who took up land in West Sechelt prior to World War One and brought his English bride Ella to Sechelt to settle after his army service, was another pioneer who worked the land for agricultural purposes.

W.J. Wakefield was engaged primarily in mixed farming on land beside the creek in West Sechelt, where he kept chickens, cows and pigs. In the summer of 1915 Mr. Wakefield's neighbours laid com-

The Whitaker cart beside the Whitaker barn, 1900–1906.

56

Jiro (Jim) Konishi and his wife Hanna at their Porpoise Bay farm some time in the 1930s.

When Charles Bradbury took this photo, circa 1913, he captioned it "A day's shooting, near Sechelt, BC" The deer and bear lying on the outer end of Bert Whitaker's wharf on Trail Bay were shot by Chief George of the Sechelt Indian band. The large nameplate on the dock could be seen from a considerable distance by people aboard steamships approaching the village. The little dog standing atop the bear was the faithful pet of Isobel Whitaker, Bert's young daughter. The man leaning against the shed was the storekeeper at Whitaker's general store.

plaints against him because his pigs were destroying their vegetable patches. The pigs destroyed tomatoes, cabbages and potatoes in the garden of Jane Nickson, cabbages and carrots at Fred Deal's home and other produce at the J. McIntyre and W. J. Gugin properties.

There were some settlers, though, who farmed on a more professional basis. About 1913 Jiro "Jim" Konishi's wife came out from Japan and together they built up a real working farm on the west side of Porpoise Bay waterfront, aided by their three sons and daughter Aggie. Jim Konishi sold fruits and vegetables and milk, delivered to the customer's door, and was also involved in the fishing industry on Sechelt Inlet. By 1938 he was proprietor of the Settlers' Supply House, which he built in Selma Park.

The Whitaker holdings included a farm, which featured a dairy stock to produce milk for the hotel. Ada Dawe recalled that in 1912 and 1913 she used to carry an empty, covered milk pail from her home to the kitchen of the Whitaker Hotel. There the Chinese cook would fill the pails of various customers. On one occasion Ada went to pass the time of day with friends in the hotel sitting room while waiting for the milk. Suddenly there was a great noise in the kitchen, caused by the cook when he took the lid off Ada's pail and two or three frogs jumped out at him. Eric Carlson—who managed the dairy herd—and his companions had conspired to set up the joke.

The Whitaker farm also produced some of the vegetables and fruits used in the hotel; the thickly clustered homes north of the present oil tanks on Wharf Road are set down in the midst of what used to be the farm orchard. The farm had a barn in which animals were slaughtered and Whitaker's horses kept.

Samuel Stanley Delong the elder and his wife with their belled cow and log barn in West Sechelt, 1919. During 1915 Sam Delong (1867–1939) pre-empted District Lot 4307, 40.6 acres on the east side of Mason Road and above Norwest Bay Road. His son, Samuel Stanley Delong the younger, pre-empted the adjoining District Lot 4310 at the same time. The senior Delongs were parents of seven children, including Stan, Bob and Lin, who logged areas of the Sunshine Coast for many years. Lin and his brother Jim walked along a logging road to attend school at Porpoise Bay.

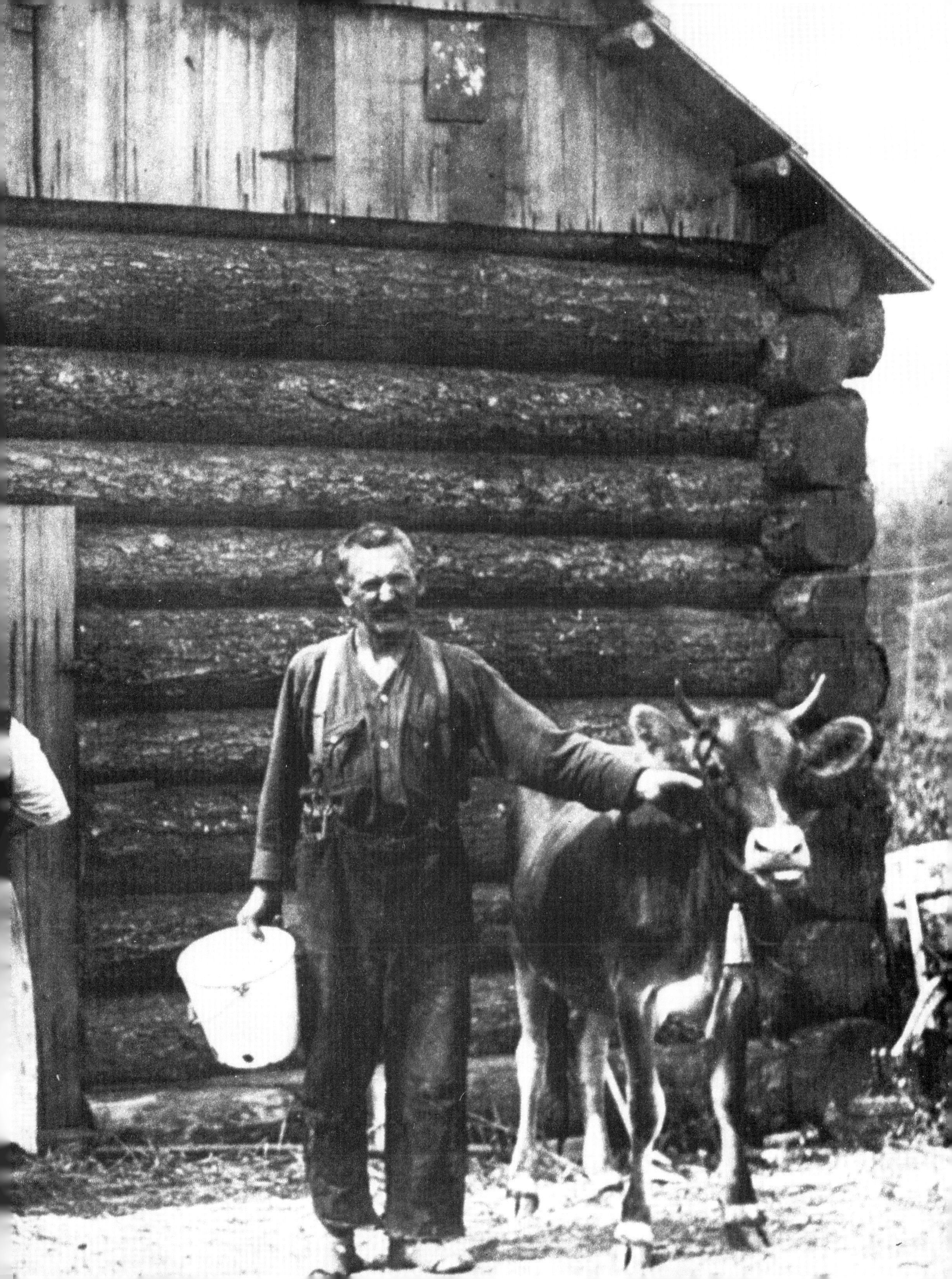

There were also some farms opened up for pre-emption in 1915 in West Sechelt—an area which had previously been held in reserve and logged over— some of which still remain intact near the upper end of what is now Mason Road.

Cows roamed freely along the road-sides and through bush in Sechelt during the early days and the bells permitted the children of the various families to retrieve their livestock. They also seemed able to predict a change in the weather; if one saw them near the beach, rain would follow.

The Tug *Commodore*

BEFORE RADIO TELEPHONES were installed in ships and before weather forecasts were readily available in outlying areas, it was commonplace to see large groups of tugs sheltering day after day in the lee of the Trail Islands or Southeast Rock while waiting for calm seas to ensure a reasonably safe passage for log booms en route to the lower mainland.

The tugs' crews spent their leisure time visiting back and forth, trading magazines and books, eating heartily, playing poker and painting the names of their tugs artistically on the local rocks. The mate of the tug *Stormer* collected botanical specimens from Trail Island. Occasionally a tug's crew tied her logs to a rock and steamed into the Sechelt wharf to pick up supplies. Or she might send a telegram message from the government office in the village; telegrams were cheap and telephones were relatively rare.

The seamen considered it a special treat when one of the Sechelt settlers gave them issues of the *Vancouver Province*. Local residents received the newspapers only two or three times a week. Tuesday's Union Steamship vessel was particularly welcome at Sechelt because it brought both the Saturday and Monday papers, with stories of human interest, elections, wars and so on not then available via early catswhisker or battery radios.

Pharic Honeyman recalled the tugs: "Trail Islands were always a spot for us to make our way to. Many a piece of pie did we kids 'cadge' from the tugboat cooks. Johnny Cook was a real sailor. He owned a sixteen-foot boat that he kept in such immaculate shape that it spelled navy all over. Well Johnny figured the best way to get to Vancouver was to await his chance, and when he noted that a tug with a boom was about to move out, generally in the evening, he would row out and tag on the end of the boom and thus was towed all the way to Vancouver. I think he probably had to row or sail all the way back to Sechelt because in those days outboard motors were few and far between."

The tug *Commodore* was for many years a member of this marine community. When the old wooden-hulled steam bessel was built in 1907 she was the largest and most powerful tug in BC waters. Moodyville Mill, North Vancouver, constructed her for BC Mills Timber and Trading Company, better know as the Hastings Mill Company. Her dimensions were 119.6 by 26.1 by 14.5 feet, with a capacity of 216.19 registered tons or 321 gross tons. She was powered by a triple expansion engine and she raised steam by burning coal. Her design was excellent, her lines were graceful, her engines quiet and her Chinese cook served superlative meals. The *Commodore*'s logs were long, straight, and huge in circumference compared with some of the crooked,

skinny specimens that wash ashore today as escapees from booms. The prime timber was beautiful and sweet-smelling.

Fraser Rock, located in Welcome Pass, east of South Thormanby Island, has been the scene of more than one shipwreck. During the evening of December 14, 1955, when she was en route to pick up a log tow, the *Commodore Straits* (as the tug was renamed) ran aground on Fraser Reef. Following are excerpts from the *Vancouver Province* story published the following day:

Ten men were rescued from the sinking tug *Commodore Straits* Wednesday night without getting their feet wet... The men were whisked off the deck of the stricken vessel, transferred from the rescue tug *Nanaimo Clipper* to another boat, and were on the way back to Vancouver—all inside an hour. First call from the *Commodore Straits* skipper, Al Bachen...was

The ill-fated tug *Commodore* (later *Commodore Straits*) in Vancouver Harbour.

461:- Pulling Out.   Vancouver B.C

heard at 9:48 p.m. His 120-foot, 48 year-old boat had struck Fraser Reef and was jammed on it going down by the stern.

After the rescue the 10 were transferred to the *Johnstone Straits*, which brought them back to Vancouver. Salvage operations were started early today when the *Salvage Queen* and the *Johnstone Straits* took two heavy lifting derricks to the spot.

The *Vancouver Sun* continued the story in its issue of December 16, 1955. "Two divers were underwater this morning surveying the sunken tub *Commodore Straits*... She is lying on her port side with her stern in 110 feet of water and her bow four feet below surface, resting on the steep incline of Fraser Reef." By Monday, December 19, the *Sun* noted that the *Commodore Straits* "slipped down into 150 feet of water Sunday and has settled on bottom upside down." Ron Johnstone, a Sechelt merchant, did some diving in the area some years later with the hope of being able to make movies and still photographs of the wreck. He observed that the *Commodore Straits*' propeller is gone and that there is a hole in the hull, which may have been blasted to gain access to the condenser. Ron measured the depth of the *Commodore Straits*' bow at 145 feet and the stern at 105 feet, when calculated at a three- or four-foot tide.

Neil Whitaker of Garden Bay, while scuba diving with Bryan Wright in September 1974, brought to the surface a relic from the *Commodore Straits*. This memento was a teredo-eaten, rust-stained block of wood with a metal bolt through it and large flake of green paint still attached. Neil presented the fragment to his aunt, Ada Dawe, widow of the man who was the mate of the *Commodore* almost sixty years before. Bryan Wright, a native of Gibsons, collected an old door and a lockset.

HUNTING AND FISHING

IT WAS COMMON around the turn of the century for hunters to bring game to the general store in Sechelt to sell. It was legal to sell venison in stores and Bert Whitaker purchased much of it from professional hunters, then shipped it to his wholesale fish and game business in Vancouver. He also sent hides and furs to his brother Ernest Whitaker, who exported raw furs and skins from Vancouver. On November 7, 1906, the Sechelt Trading Company purchased from J. Wilson one deer, 107 pounds (actual weight 127 pounds) for $5.35. A few days later on November 11 Mr. Wilson sold one deer, 95 pounds (actual weight 120 pounds) for $4.75. This works out to a price of five cents per pound of dressed venison. In his book *The Trail of Chack Chack*, Harry Roberts writes of rows of deer carcasses he observed hanging on the steamer going to town.

Trout caught from Clowhom Lake, up Sechelt Inlet, in the span of two hours in 1942.

A fishing boat passes in front of the Indian village, circa 1920s or 1930s.

Fish were abundant in the pioneer days in Sechelt, and many settlers fished in the same way they farmed, as a supplement to their own provisions. The BC Fishing and Trading Company was established in 1892 at Rowland Point near Skookum Chuk, and a number of professional fishermen worked in the area around Pender Harbour. Yamamoto Boat Works was established at the head of Porpoise Bay in the first decade of the century to service fishing boats, before the building became the site of the second Sechelt school in 1913. The Sechelt Indian Band fished as well. Clarence Joe once recalled that the steamship *Camosun I* used to stop at the Sechelt wharf on Trail Bay and take almost the entire population of the Indian village, including the children, north to Rivers Inlet. Jean Whitaker remembered that the mass exodus took place during the summer vacation periods in the 1920s. The Sechelt women worked in the canneries and the men fished. The *Camosun* called at the canneries to bring down fish and crews. Finally, the establishment of Sechelt and Selma Park as resorts brought an increasing number of sports fishermen to the area.

The whaling steamer *St. Lawrence* off Sechelt in April 1919. Note the cannon on the bow and the inflated carcass alongside the ship. When an animal was secured it was inflated with air so that it could easily be towed ashore for flensing.

The Whaling Steamer *St. Lawrence*

KILLER WHALES are often observed along the Sunshine Coast and fortunate tourists may see one or two frolicking not far off the ferry running between Horseshoe Bay and Langdale. Residents who spot the sea mammals through living room windows happily phone their neighbours around the next point to give welcome news that spouting signs should soon be visible.

Circumstances were much less hospitable during the year 1908 when the steamer *St. Lawrence* broke the world's whaling record. Operating from Kyoquot she slaughtered 318 whales, including 241 humpbacks, 66 sulphur bottoms, 10 finbacks and one sperm whale. Previous to that time flensing stations had been set up in Georgia Strait at Whaletown on Cortez Island and at Pasley Island in the entrance to Howe Sound. On the latter site huge piles of bone accumulated when the blubber was stripped from the carcasses. Whale bones could be used to temper steel or stiffen ladies' corsets. Pioneer settlers were familiar with large pods of whales which frequented the area from Bowen Island up past Gibsons into Pender Harbour and on by way of Jervis Inlet down Sechelt Inlet into Porpoise Bay.

MINING

THE MINISTER OF MINES' REPORT for 1920 indicated a fair number of claims located in different localities: Halfmoon Bay 5, Sechelt and Porpoise Bay 13, Mc-Nabb Creek and Valley 19, Narrows Arm 8, Egmont 8 and Salmon Inlet 7. It also mentioned "the Tyzoone River section, which flows into the head of Narrows Arm in Sechelt Inlet, where Ben Coates with four assistants has located about seventy claims as agents for a number of miners, residents of Vancouver."

The most significant mining operation in the Sechelt area, though, was that operated by T.R. Nickson. Thomas Ralph Nickson was well known locally in 1912 and 1913 as president of Nickson and Company, general contractors, as well as its subsidiaries, Sechelt Granite Quarries and Canadian Builders' Supply Company, which employed from one hundred to six hundred men at all times, chiefly in Vancouver. He was a son of John Joseph Nickson and his wife Jane, who with most of their large family took up residence on the Trail Bay waterfront about 1904. Ralph brought stonecutters to Sechelt to quarry granite from an area just above Highway 101 and east of Norwest Bay Road. The stones were transported downhill in a dolly on tracks, which were supported by a rock cribbing still visible in 1983. At the beach the stones were loaded on scows and towed to the Fraser River, where they were finished and used between the streetcar tracks on Vancouver thoroughfares.

Thomas Ralph Nickson, owner of Sechelt Granite Quarries. He was a son of John Joseph and Jane Nickson, who with most of their large family took up residence on the Trail Bay waterfront about 1904.

Nickson obtained a contract to supply rock for the breakwater at Victoria and he used Sechelt granite for the purpose, but ultimately he found the Sunshine Coast too far distant so he found another source. He removed the quarry equipment and never brought it back. Remnants of cut stone were still observable on the shoreline as late as 1982, and local homes have chimneys, fireplaces and wells constructed from stones salvaged after the quarry was abandoned.

Today another major quarry operation exists on the Sechelt Indian Band Lands. Though the equipment is different, the idea is the same as the old Nickson quarry, with a conveyor transporting gravel across Highway 101 to the waterfront, where it can be loaded directly onto barges.

Quarried granite blocks from the 1912 Sechelt Granite Quarries operation left on the beach below the junction of the Sunshine Coast Highway and Norwest Bay Road.

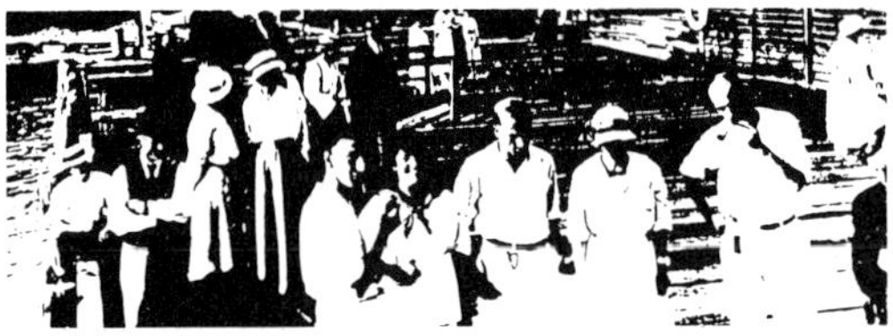

RESORTS

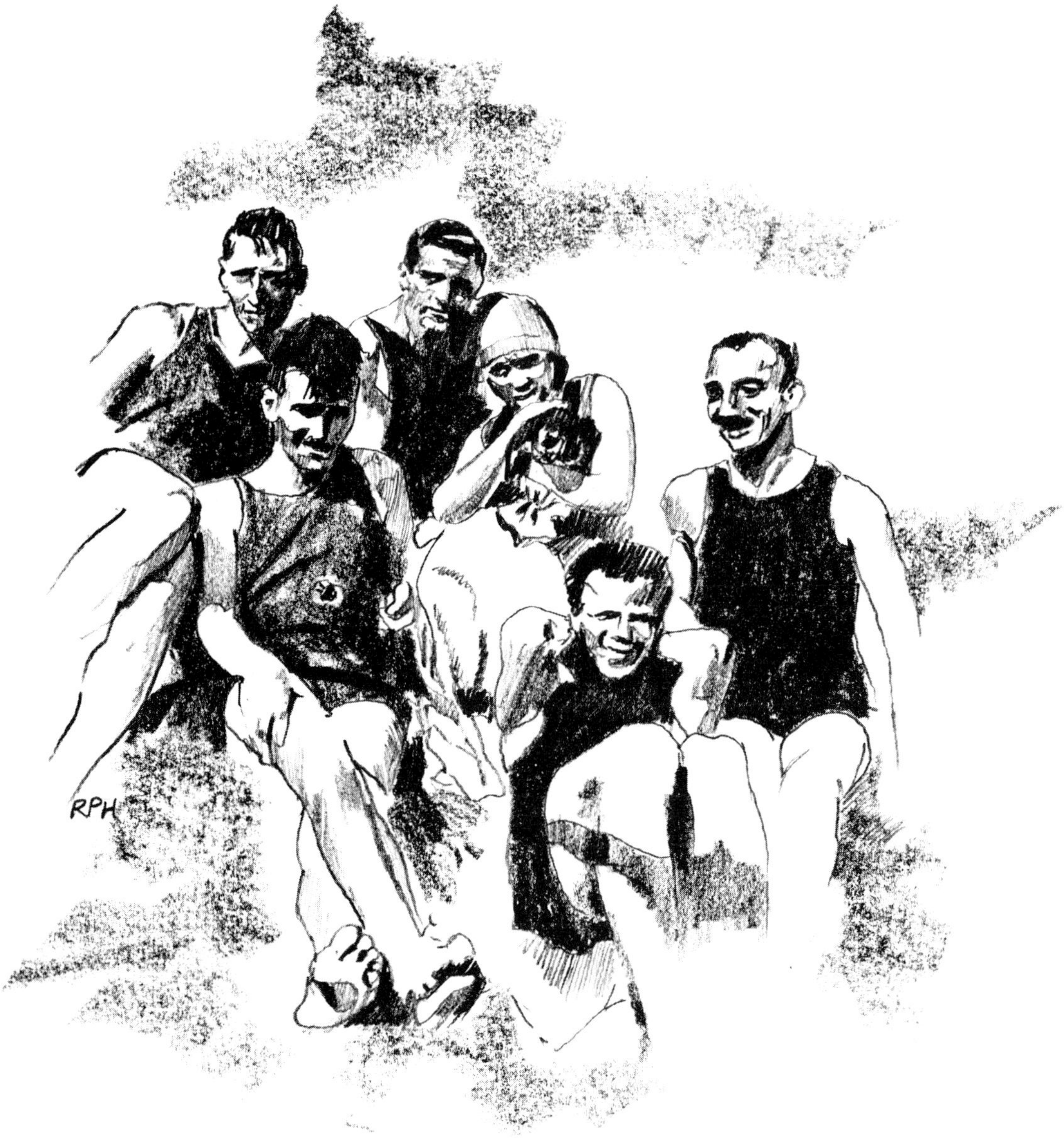
RPH

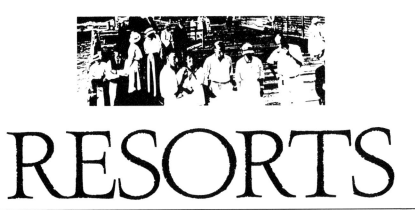

THE WHITAKER HOTELS

THE EARLIEST ACCOMMODATION in Sechelt for workers and tourists alike was provided by Bert Whitaker with the establishment of the first Sechelt Hotel on the west side of Porpoise Bay Road near the approach to the wharf. Sam Dawe recalls the hotel: "It was a two-storied building with large verandahs at both levels, constructed in 1899 by Mr. Whitaker. During the summer $35.00 to $50.00 per month. Out of season rates were often lower when the hotel accommodated transient workmen. Printed in a box at the head of each page of the register was a notice reading: "For hire: steam launches and rowboats."

Before long Mr. Whitaker's establishment was an attractive tourist draw. In 1902 the Canadian Pacific Navigation Company wrote to Bert Whitaker expressing its intention "to run an excur-

Buildings on the Boulevard between Inlet Avenue and the Indian reserve, owned by Bert Whitaker and photographed almost certainly in 1906. Left to right: (1) First hotel, prior to the addition of a large wing on the west end, with a fence to keep out sheep; (2) second store and post office; (3) first store and post office; (4) first barn; (5) third store and post office. A woman who travelled with her brothers to Sechelt as a child at the turn of the century once told me that her brothers amused themselves by "fishing" for bats off the balcony of the hotel. Their fishlines were baited with food and when cast over the railing actually succeeded in catching bats.

months the guests were mostly people on holiday from Vancouver and more distant places." The original structure contained twenty guest rooms, and about another eighteen rooms were added around 1906–07.

It is interesting to note the hotel rates as recorded in the old register. Depending upon the location and size of the rooms the prices ranged from $2.00 to $2.50 per day, $10.00 to $15.00 per week and

Guests in front of Bert Whitaker's first Sechelt Hotel on the Boulevard at the south end of Inlet Avenue between 1900 and 1904.

The general store, wharf and hotel in the late 1920s or early 1930s.

GENERAL STORE

4.

HOTEL and BEACH
SECHELT, B.C.

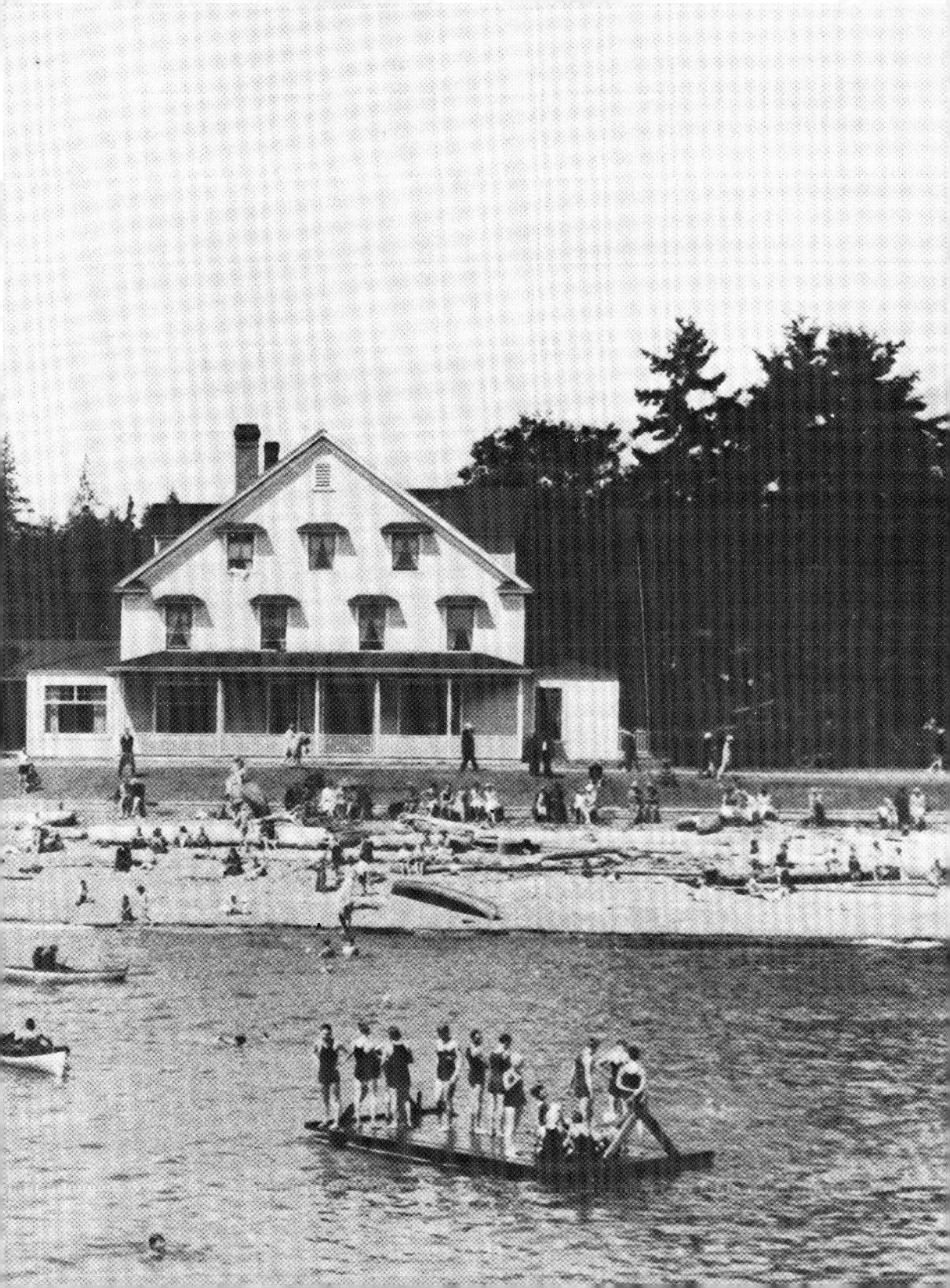

Bert Whitaker pushes a boatload of luggage, hotel guests and others off the beach as they are ferried out to board the Union Steamship *Comox*, lying in Trail Bay. The date of the photo is between 1906 and 1910.

sion to Sechelt on July 1, 1902 by the steamer *Yosemite*." The firm stated its presumption that Whitaker's "raft or float is in good condition to handle a large crowd without danger of any accidents." Newspaper ads in Vancouver enticed people celebrating the national birthday to take a trip aboard the paddlewheeler *Yosemite*; they could pay $1 return to sail for Sechelt at 10 a.m. or pay 50 cents for a moonlight excursion from 8 to 11 p.m.

Sam Dawe remembers:

> ...the attempt to mix tourism with loggers was not always too successful. Inasmuch as Mr. Whitaker at one time operated five logging and some shinglebolt camps in or near Sechelt Inlet, there were at times a number of loggers around the hotel. In those days before prohibition the hotel boasted a very fine bar with a beautiful view over the straits. At times it became somewhat rowdy, which was not greatly to the liking of some of the summer people.

In the winter, the people on vacation were scarce but in their place were men, and some of their wives, from a stone quarry operated by Mr. T.R. Nickson. The quarry was engaged in getting out paving stones for Vancouver streets and was situated approximately two miles west of Sechelt.

The road, such as it was, ended about where the Shop-Easy parking lot is now. The route for getting to Sechelt from the west was a trail which followed more or less the

A view down the beach at Trail Bay from the original location of Rock Cottage, which is in the forground on the left. Visible farther down is Beach House and Our Lady of Lourdes Indian church. The photo was taken in 1912 or shortly thereafter.

The Sechelt Wharf on Trail Bay in 1912 with Capt. Thomas Patrick O'Kelly and six members of the Sechelt Indian nation displaying salmon for the purpose of enticing sportsmen to the area. Tourist promotion methods have scarcely altered during the intervening years. Capt. O'Kelly (1877–1948) was associated with the Sechelt Hotel, served as postmaster at Sechelt in 1914 and as a School Trustee in 1915.

Fashionable sportswear while fishing in rainforest country circa 1910. The young women displaying their catch are standing on Sechelt's Trail Bay pebbles in front of Beach House. Note the serviceable binding along the edge of the long woollen skirt, also the identical oilskins, probably purchased in the Sechelt General Store. Left to right: Dolly Boult (later Mrs. Rowan), Muriel Whitaker (later the wife of Rev. Norman Thompson) and Evelyn Whitaker (later Mrs. Haslett). The two Whitaker girls were the daughters of Alfred and Henrietta Whitaker.

contours of the beach and passed within about a dozen feet from the back door of T.J. Cook.

Every evening men from the quarry came in to the hotel, where there was a large sitting room, and on most nights a party naturally ensued. Some of the workers at the quarry came from Wales, a country famed for its fine singers, and their considerable talents furnished entertainment for all. Jack Davis, stoker on the *Tartar*, was also a Welshman and his songs were received with particular favour.

There were a number of ladies living in Sechelt at the time: Miss Grace Kent, the schoolteacher; Miss Muriel Denham, Miss Amelia James and another young lady, who were employed at the hotel; several of the wives of the stonecutters; Miss Ada Cook, who later became my wife; and others. The bartender at the hotel was Teddy Sweet and the storekeeper was Mr. Tait, who was assisted by Jim Konishi. Eric Carlson, teamster for Mr. Whitaker, also looked after the dairy stock. The balance of the population was made up on loggers and the occasional traveller.

Always on Saturday nights, and sometimes more often, there was an impromptu dance. People from Gibsons travelled on the *Tartar* to the Saturday night dances. There was a road of sorts between Gibsons and Sechelt, but only for horse and wagon, so that visitors travelling by land had to ford Mission Creek as

The Sechelt Hotel with fire burning through its roof on June 1, 1914. Many volunteers fought the blaze but water pressure was so inadequate that only ashes remained. The tide was ebbing when fire erupted, so rescued mattresses and furniture were carried to the beach where a horse and wagon picked them up.

A bucket brigade at work on the telegraph office (also used at various times as a store, school and bunkhouse) while the hotel burns in the background.

6. Sechelt Hotel Fire, 1 June, 1914

Furniture from the first hotel sitting on the beach after it was saved from the fire in 1914. The hotel kitchen range was set up on Trail Bay beach and bread was baked in its oven.

third hotel under the name of the Sechelt Inn.

THE SECHELT INN

THE THREE-STOREY SECHELT INN was known as Beach House when it was built for Alfred and Henrietta Whitaker in 1905–06, on the Boulevard where the Driftwood Inn stands now. It contained seven bedrooms. The Union Steamship Company purchased the private home in 1926 and operated it as a hotel annex and later as the Sechelt Inn until 1952, when they sold the business to Florence "Manny" Duncan. She managed the hotel successfully for a decade before a fire on July 20, 1963 rendered the building uninhabitable. As a safety measure the firemen deliberately set a second fire the following year, reducing the inn to ashes.

there was no bridge at that time.

The *Tartar* always stayed at the wharf if possible, but sometimes the weather was so bad we had to leave. When it was blowing a gale and dark we did not attempt to go to the buoy; instead we steamed back and forth along the shore off Selma Park and Davis Bay.

The hotel burned down in 1914, and Mr. Whitaker's first store building was converted into the second hotel, which in turn was destroyed by fire in 1937. After the second fire the building which had been Mr. Whitaker's home became the

Bert Whitaker had also erected several cottages on the waterfront for the purpose of renting them to vacationing families from Vancouver. Two of them are still in existence: Rock Cottage near Snickett Park and another house on the Boulevard known variously as Kwitcherkicken, Killarney or Green Cottage.

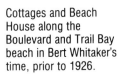

Cottages and Beach House along the Boulevard and Trail Bay beach in Bert Whitaker's time, prior to 1926.

The Sechelt Inn, formerly Beach House, some time between 1952 and 1963.

UNION RESORTS

IN OCTOBER 1917 the Union Steamship Company purchased the ships and property of the All Red Line, which had established a resort at Selma Park dating back to before the First World War. The new owners immediately set to work to expand facilities and attract an increased volume of excursion groups and vacationers who would travel on Union vessels.

Cottages supplied with water were built at Selma Park and made ready for occupancy by the spring of 1919. These were of two types, described in a company brochure as "cottage bungalows and camp cottages." Tent accommodation was also available. Children and their mothers would often spend a month or a season in a rented cottage, while the fathers joined them on weekends free from their Vancouver jobs. The men travelled on the Union "daddy boats," so called because the children crowded the wharves along the Sunshine Coast to wave and call out, "Goodbye, Daddy" as the Sunday Union vessels transported the

The Boulevard, Sechelt, circa late 1920s or early 1930s. The revenue cottage on the left was built by Bert Whitaker. The Union Steamship Company erected the three identical cottages in the centre and also constructed the concrete seawall on the cobble beach in the foreground. Storms subsequently destroyed the western portion of the breakwater, but about 80 feet of it still remains intact, though barely visible, in front of Royal Terraces and the Parthenon Restaurant.

The dance pavilion at Selma Park, built in 1920 by the Union Steamship Company on the "Fill" above the highway. When the hall was illuminated on a summer's evening it appeared very beautiful, especially while the music of dance bands imported from Vancouver wafted on the air.

Selma Park beach back in the days when the clinker-built rowboat was a popular means of transportation on Trail Bay. There are 13 such craft in this view. Observe the ladies in long dresses, children balancing on crude rafts, the retaining wall and the beautiful arbutus trees.

breadwinners away from the fishing, swimming and other recreation back to their toil in the city.

In 1920 a dance hall was opened across the highway from the Selma Park wharf and the new general store there, in an area known as the "Fill." Jessie M. Van der Burg prepared a history of the Union Steamship Company up to 1943, wherein she described the Selma Park dance pavilion as follows:

The pavilion was built high up on the slope and from it one could have a magnificent view of the Gulf Islands. The floor was 60 feet long by 36 feet wide and was a fine dancing floor. This pavilion, together with other attractions of the place, made the resort very popular. The new ship *Capilano* provided a semi-weekly service, with special trips on Sunday.

A tea room functioned on the spacious verandah across the front of the pavilion. During the warm evenings long before public electric power was available lo-

A crowd of picnickers streams off the Trail Bay wharf on their way to the picnic grounds in what is probably the 1930s.

cally, the verandah was handsome in the light of primitive lamps, while the sound of music carried from the floor.

One of the tourist leaflets issued by the Union Steamship Company in the late 1920s described Selma's attractions in a vocabulary and style worth quoting:

The ramblage in the vicinity of Selma is charming and there is a splendid dance pavilion, commanding one of the most glorious seaviews on the coast. Every outdoor recreation is immediately available — bathing (with good facilities), boating, fishing (first-rate salmon trolling in the bay) and tennis. Spacious picnic grounds, with all facilities for sports and refreshments are at the disposal of picnic parties throughout the summer. This is a good centre for hikes, Selma lying within a mile of Sunny Sechelt.

In April 1926 the Union company purchased the Whitaker properties at Sechelt and soon erected another pavilion there. Dances were then held on summer Saturday nights, one week at Selma Park and the alternate week at Sechelt. These sites provided recreation for the huge parties of up to two thousand people which the Union ships transported to Sechelt and Selma Park. Sometimes three boats — the *Lady Alexandra*, *Lady Cynthia* and *Lady Cecilia* — came into the Sechelt wharf in quick succession and discharged passengers simultaneously from both upper and lower decks, with fore and aft gangways. The vessels then sped away to take other jobs before returning to Sechelt in time to carry the picnickers home at 7 p.m. In those days office staffs commonly worked on Saturday mornings and could not leave the city on Friday evenings for their country weekends.

The St. John's Ambulance Society sent attendants as well since there was no resident physician at Sechelt until Dr. Holm arrived in 1939.

A band always accompanied the larger picnics to provide music aboard the boats and at the park. The Liberal Party picnic at Sechelt on July 5, 1939 brought along the Vancouver Junior Band of sixty

Holiday makers on the Trail Bay beach in 1916, with the third general store in the background and the second hotel on the right.

pieces. Sometimes the bands came upcoast from Vancouver on the Saturday afternoon boat and returned to town on Sunday, playing en route. Musicians who performed in the local dance halls included Bert Scott of Roberts Creek, Frank Bolney and the well-known Rhythm Pals. The bandsmen I remember wore white flannel trousers with black and yellow striped blazers. One of the orchestras was known as the Sechelters.

Large employers like Woodward's, Hudson's Bay and BC Electric would annually close shop for a day and take entire staffs on excursions to Bowen Island or the Sunshine Coast. These happy folk with their families and friends sailed from Vancouver at 9 a.m. and arrived at Sechelt shortly after 11. Local children were attracted to the wharf to watch the visiting hordes stream ashore and take over the village. Some headed to the beach to enjoy swimming, boating or fishing. Others proceeded directly to the picnic grounds where the grass was furnished with very long, heavy tables and benches. The park stoves were already lit

to provide hot water for tea and coffee. Ice cream and fruit were given free to the children, but picnickers usually brought their own sandwiches.

The more sophisticated guests could dine at the hotel or partake of refreshments at the Totem Tea Room in the dance pavilion on the waterfront. The general store, although large, was overcrowded with souvenir seekers.

Large sports programs were arranged, including foot races, a tug of war and a baseball game. These excursions continued until the Depression years, changes in the style of logging camps and the coming of the Second World War all affected the Union Steamship Company adversely. In 1944 they sold their Selma Park property. The picnic ground property at Sechelt was placed in trust for a park in 1952, and the dance pavilion there was sold in 1954.

Mr. and Mrs. Livingstone were operating the former Selma Park dance hall as Totem Lodge when it was destroyed by fire early one Sunday morning, April 6, 1952. The volunteer fire brigade fought 77

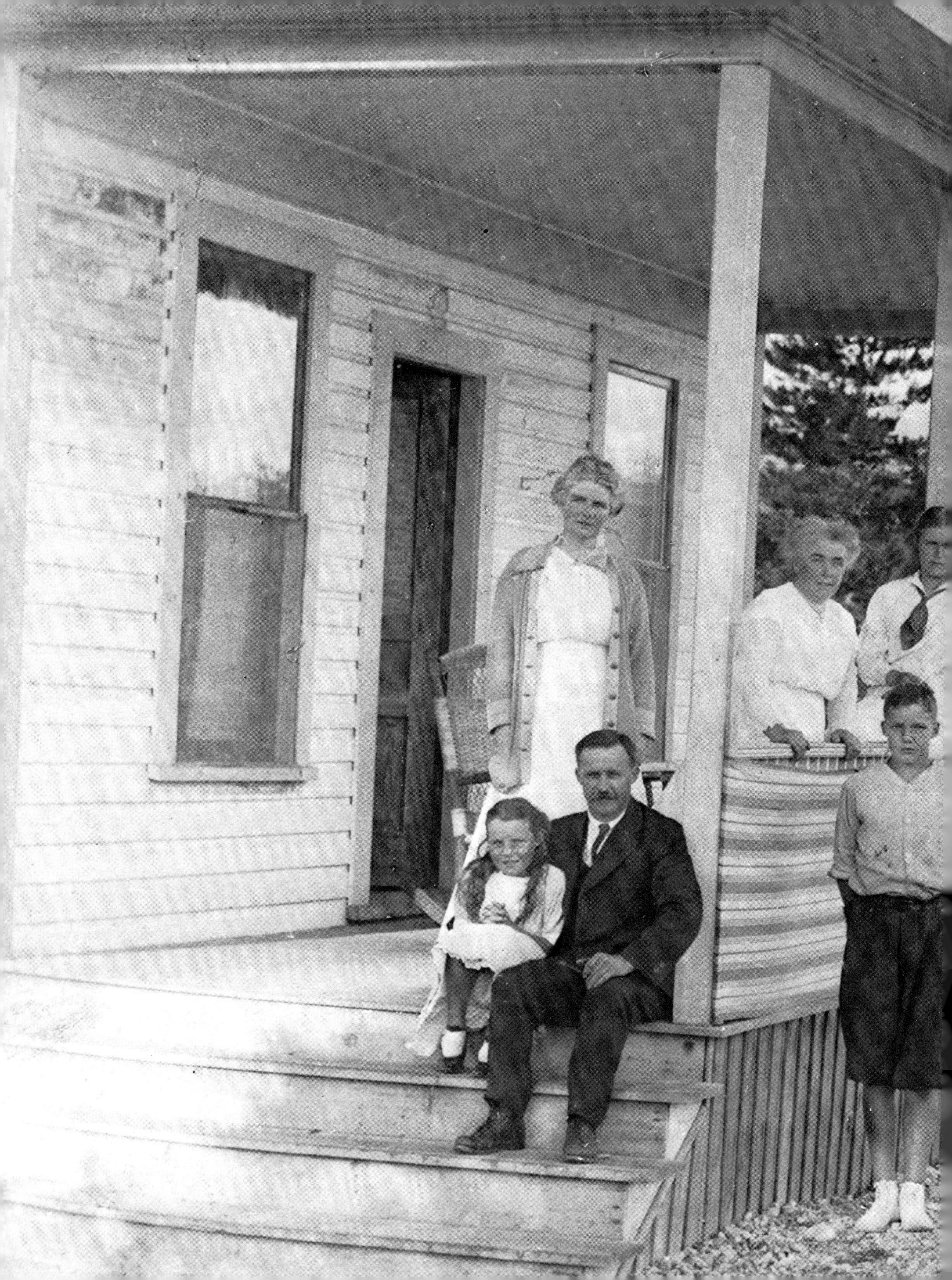

One of the Trail Bay waterfront cottages, with Beach House in the background.

the blaze, but because a high wind was blowing they could do nothing to save the old landmark from becoming a ruin within half an hour. Mr. William G. "Red" McBean burned to death in the fire. Fortunately the Livingstone family and other occupants of the building escaped and Sechelt firemen were able to prevent the flames from spreading to nearby houses.

The Sechelt Dance Pavilion survived variously as a movie theatre, salal plant, and private dwelling until May 27, 1971, when it too suffered a severe fire.

OTHER ACCOMMODATION

THERE WERE, in addition to the Union resorts, individuals in Sechelt and Selma Park offering accommodation from a relatively early date. By the 1930s one only needed to read the classified ads in the Vancouver papers during the month of June to see long lists of furnished summer beachside cottages and campsites offered for rent from Redrooffs through West Sechelt, Sechelt, Selma Park, Davis Bay and Roberts Creek. In Selma Park in the 1930s there was Bayview Lodge and Sunset Inn. Opeongo Lodge was built by Bryce and Gertrude Fleck in 1926 on

waterfront property at the intersection of Teredo Street and Shorncliffe Avenue, known for over half a century as Fleck's Corner. In 1968 this lodge was purchased by Captain Gordon Jones and his wife Myheera, who employed Norman Franklin and Al Gibbons to modernize it, though a forty-five-year-old wooden-decked tennis court from the original estate was battered into nothingness by modern heavy equipment during efforts to render Highway 101 at Fleck's Corner safer for traffic in 1975. At the same time the old planting of beech, oak and laburnum trees on the site was destroyed, breaking another link with the past.

Other accommodation in the area in the late 1930s included Glendalough, the home of Jack and Carrie Mayne, which can still be seen at the corner of Inlet Avenue and Cowrie Street, and Rockwood Lodge, opened in 1936 by William and Jessie Youngson.

The Youngsons were Scottish people who came to the village in 1926. Jessie was a superlative cook as well as a skillful and enthusiastic gardener. The meals she served and the beautiful landscaping she and Bill achieved attracted vacationers as well as hydro and highway crews, travelling salesmen and all manner of govern-

Bryce Fleck (centre in dark jacket) standing on his private boat-launching slip on the Trail Bay beach in 1927. The concrete marine ways were equipped with rails upon which a dolly holding the boat was winched up into the boat house. The granite bluff on the left is named Fleck's Rocks. The children (left to right) are Betty Fleck (MD), Drew Fleck, Nancy Fleck and Janet Fleck (Mrs. Ladner), with Betty Youngson (Mrs. Ingram) in the stern. Since the turn of the century kids have been high-diving off these rocks, children have caught shiners and rock cod there, and the wild otter still brings his freshly-caught fish dinner to be eaten on the small reef adjoining. Waves on the beach wrecked the ramp long ago but remnants of the rails were still observable at low tide in the early 1980s.

Rockwood Lodge, which opened for business on July 27, 1936 is now considered a heritage building. Here we see construction under way in 1935, when the rockeries and bridge across the fish pond were already in place.

William Alexander Youngson and his daughter Betty (later Mrs. Ingram of Vancouver) photographed in 1927 beside the Opeongo Lodge truck. Bill was born in Scotland on July 11, 1889. He brought his wife and their child to live in Sechelt in 1926, when he was employed by the Bryce Fleck family. The back of the truck was enclosed in wire to prevent the four Fleck children from falling out when Bill drove them along the rough roads of the day. He also transported guests from the Union Steamship boats to Opeongo Lodge. In 1935–36 the Youngson family built Rockwood Lodge. Bill was a qualified mechanic whose garage at the foot of the Rockwood driveway was converted into a tourist booth in 1982. Mr. Youngson died in 1968 and his ashes are buried in the cemetery next door to Rockwood.

ment officials. Indeed Rockwood came to be known as "Government House" because of the politicians, school inspectors, assessors, police officers and the like who found a home away from home at the lodge. The Youngsons ran Rockwood successfully for ten years. After that, it changed ownership six times between 1946 and 1980.

It was eventually bought by the Sechelt Chamber of Commerce, who used it for their own offices and operated a tea room and craft shop. The garage building became a Tourist Information Centre and continues to be so today. In 1984 they leased the building to Western Moorbad Resort, Inc., who converted the heritage lodge into a health spa and built what has now become the North Wing. The venture failed, however, and in 1986 the District of Sechelt assumed the mortgage. In 1987 the District granted permission to a local group to manage the lodge as a community use facility. They have completely restored the old building, redecorated the North Wing, established lovely rhododendron gardens and renamed the complex Rockwood Centre. It is now managed by the Suncoast Rockwood Lodge Society, which makes it available for meetings, seminars workshops and recreational activities. Every August, Rockwood Centre is also the headquarters of the successful Sechelt Festival of the Written Arts, instituted by writer Betty Keller in 1983.

COMMERCIAL AND RETAIL DEVELOPMENT

MOST EARLY RETAIL ACTIVITY in Sechelt centred around Bert Whitaker's general store. In addition to lumber and game, a customer could buy a variety of items from Whitaker's store ranging from men's or women's clothes to combs, mirrors, perfume, mouth organs, material, and a variety of toys.

From the mid-1920s until the mid-1950s commercial activity in Sechelt revolved around the Union Steamship Company holdings in the pavilion on the Boulevard, which had previously been the site of the Whitaker stores and hotels. Like the Whitaker general store, the Union store offered a variety of goods to Sechelt residents, as well as a number of services. An advertisement in the *Coast News* in 1947 said: "Ladies Dresses. A nice selection just arrived. Priced from $4.50 to $7.50." A 1951 advertisement offered bush wood and coal, as well as a "general hauling" service and a garbage disposal service. Another advertisement from the same month told readers, "We are getting a fair supply of Local Cod Fillets 39 cents lb. Bring us your soap coupons. We have a large stock from which to choose."

In the years after World War II the commercial center of Sechelt shifted inland to Cowrie Street in order to take advantage of traffic on Highway 101, which was paved in 1952. In a sense, this marked the end of an era in Sechelt. A community that was founded on access by sea was restructuring itself to accommodate access by road. And the days in which the town revolved around one company, whether it be Whitaker's holdings or the Union company, were ending.

Morgan Thompson, Jack and Lee Redman and Norman Watson became

The interior of what is probably Bert Whitaker's third store, on the east side of Wharf Avenue, circa 1913–1914. The boxes on the top shelf contained men's hats. The string hanging from the ceiling on the left was used to tie parcels and the ladder was used to reach the upper shelves before self-service was initiated. Drygoods and clothing were on one side of the store and groceries were on the opposite wall.

A section of the Trail Bay waterfront around 1926. The buildings, from left, are: the dance pavilion built by the Union company in 1926; a rear view of a house on the southeast corner of Cowrie and Inlet built by Bert Whitaker in 1900; a store built by Bert Whitaker, used also as a telegraph office and the first school, and the general store at the southwest corner of Wharf Road and the Boulevard.

THE TOTEM TEAROOMS AT SECHELT BC

involved in businesses in Sechelt in the years following World War II. The development of their enterprises provides some insight into the development and transition of the community's commercial and retail sector in these years.

MORGAN THOMPSON

MORGAN THOMPSON arrived in Sechelt from Ontario in the spring of 1954 and entered into partnership with the late Bill Parsons to operate the Sechelt Theatre and Sechelt Men's Wear. Both businesses were located in the Union Estates dance pavilion, erected in 1926 on the Boulevard between Inlet Avenue and Wharf Road. Construction work was done by Ron Whitaker and his cousin Edric Clayton. The lumber was provided by the BC Fir and Cedar Company. Immediately to the west of the pavilion stood what is now the Parthenon Restaurant, originally the Union Bath house (changing rooms), coffee shop and ice cream parlour, built at the same time.

The pavilion was enlarged in 1937 and for forty-five years contributed a great variety of services to the Sechelt community until fire destroyed the landmark on May 27, 1971. At the time of the blaze Bill and Grace Reynolds were operating the former Bath house as the Whispering Pines Restaurant and the late John Hayes owned the movie Theatre, a salal plant and a rental apartment in the pavilion. The Totem Tea Room in the building was popular. It was named for the three totem poles carved in Sechelt and erected about 1928 east of the tea room. In 1955 the Union company shipped the totems to their property on Bowen Island, much to the sorrow of Sechelt residents. Badminton was played in winter in the hall and young people enjoyed roller skating parties there.

Bill Parsons had been briefly in partnership with Jack Anderson and in early 1953 the two young men purchased Gordon West's moving picture business. Mr. West came to Sechelt after World War II and set himself up as Pacific Motion Pictures. He employed Terry Frost and Don Head as projectionists at Gibsons and Sechelt and he also ran a 16-mm circuit at Pender Harbour once a week. Gordon renovated the west end of the Sechelt pavilion by building double entrance doors at ground level. These gave access to a lobby where popcorn was sold. Stairs inside led up to perhaps a dozen rows of elevated seats. The remaining chairs were on the floor level of the pavilion. The projection booth was above the popcorn

Three totem poles standing on Sechelt's Boulevard between Inlet and Wharf Avenues were commissioned by the Union Steamship Company in 1926. They were carved near the Sechelt residential school by Paul Weenah of the Owikeno Band, Rivers Inlet. He was married to a sister of Dan Paul and the couple lived in Sechelt for a time. Paul Weenah was assisted by local carvers Dan Paul, Mike Paul and Frank Isadore (a.k.a. Frank Eugene). Circa 1928 the poles were erected by Jimmy Bogart, who worked for 52 years as a carpenter for the Union company. The totems stood between the dance pavilion built for Bert Whitaker in the first half of the 1920s (left) and his general store erected in 1899 (right). These structures were purchased by the Union company in 1926. The firm pulled out of Sechelt after the Second World War. Children climbed the poles to remove beaks, ears, etc. Repairs were made but the vandalism continued, so on April 1, 1955 the totems were shipped to Bowen Island. The whole community grieved over the loss.

stand. A Sechelt Theatre advertisement in the *Coast News* in April of 1951 tells moviegoers of some soon-to-be-appearing films: "Bing Crosby in *Riding High.* Errol Flynn in the Glorious Technicolor *The Adventures of Robin Hood.* John Wayne in *Operation Tomahawk.*"

Upon arriving in Sechelt Morgan Thompson took over as projectionist. He recalled that some minor concern arose sometimes when skunks were attracted by the warmth of the furnace in the basement of the theatre.

In 1954 Thompson and Parsons purchased the pavilion and the hundred feet of valuable waterfront property on which it stood, known as Lot 1, between Inlet Avenue and Wharf Road. The price was $10,000, paid to the Union company in Vancouver in monthly installments of $150.

On November 27, 1954, Morgan Thompson and Bill Parsons celebrated the grand opening of their new business, Sechelt Men's Wear. This was located in the centre portion of the pavilion and was

The pavilion and tennis court in the late 1920s or early 1930s.

The dance pavilion under construction in the early 1920s.

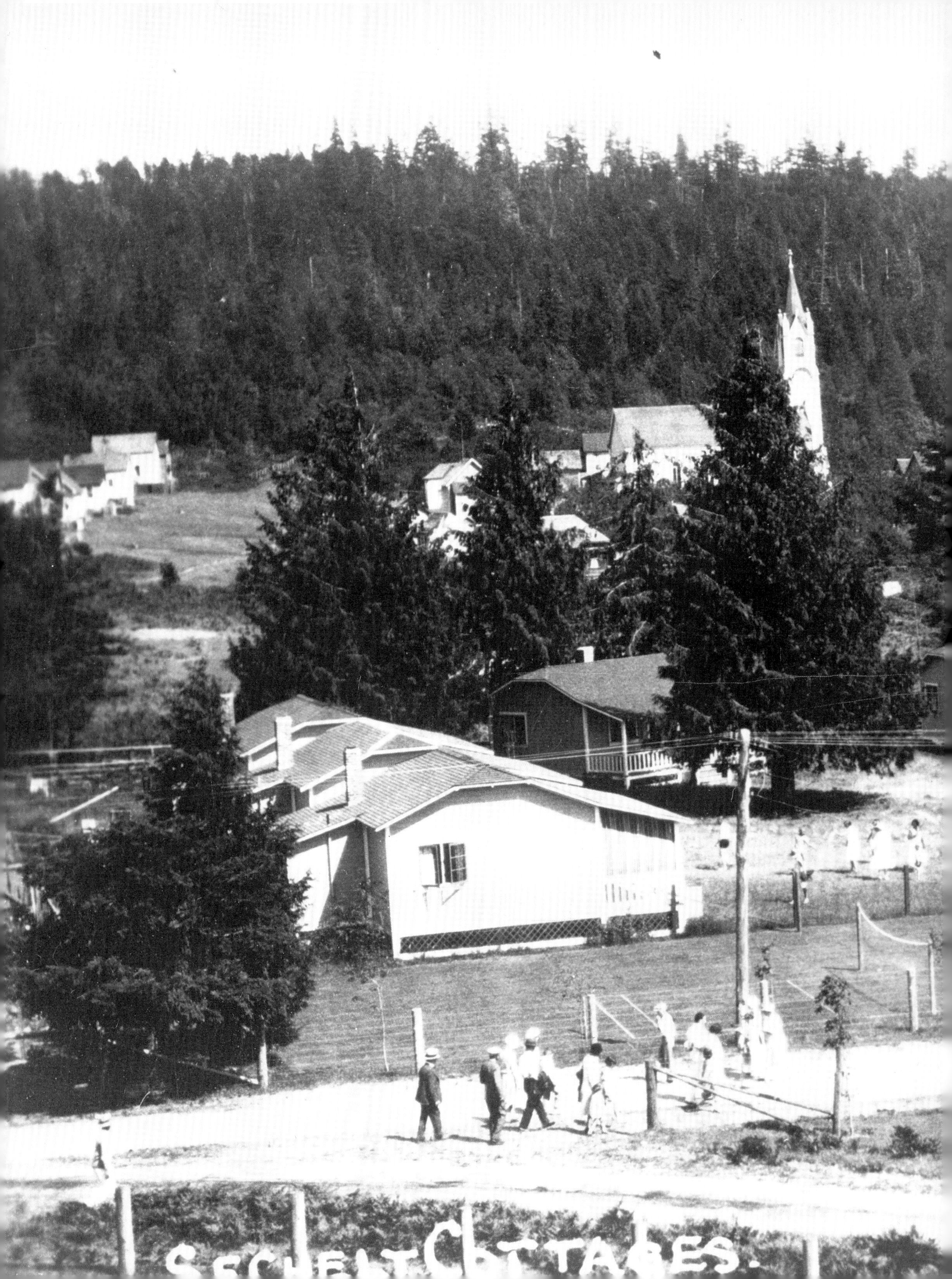
SECHELT COTTAGES.

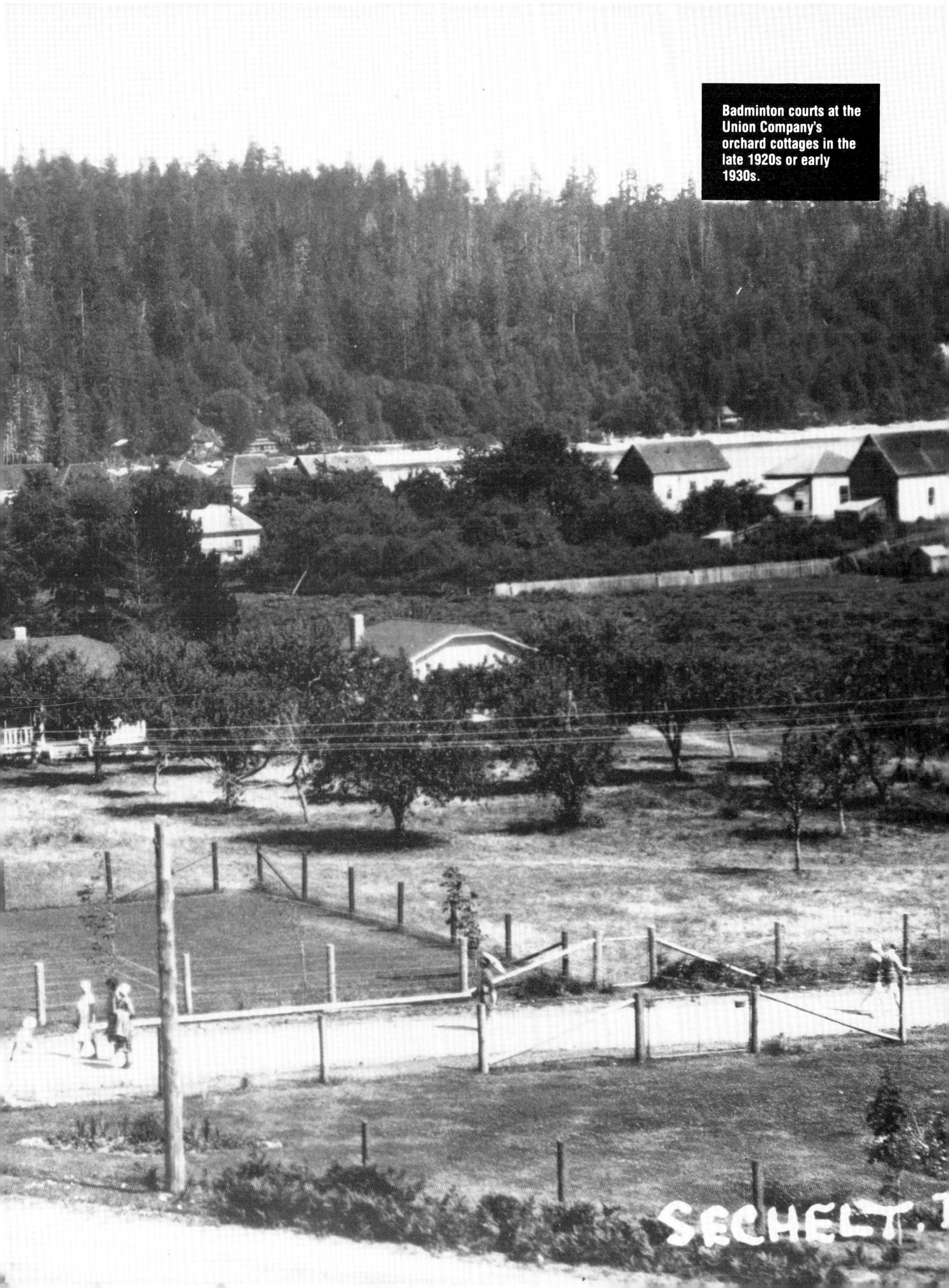
SECHELT.

Badminton courts at the Union Company's orchard cottages in the late 1920s or early 1930s.

Sechelt's commercial centre in the late 1920s.

The Union bath house and dance pavilion in 1937.

heated by a large fireplace, for which Morgan gathered logs from the beach. Thompson operated the men's wear shop in the daytime, and when he had to run the projector for the Saturday matinées, Bill came up from Vancouver and served in the store. Opening day prices in 1954 included topcoats at $19.95, doeskin work shirts at $2.95 and shorts for 49 cents a pair.

Dr. Duncan McColl's office was situated on the east side of the pavilion in space which Morgan later used as living quarters. Because many of the village men were out working in the woods, Morgan and Bill sometimes served on the coroner's jury after fatal logging accidents.

East of the pavilion stood the Sechelt wharf and the old Union general store, which had traditionally attracted business to the boulevard. The store closed in April 1956, and a year later Morgan and Bill moved their shop to Cowrie Street where the commercial centre of the village was relocating. The Union store was demolished in late 1965 and the site is now occupied by Royal Terraces.

Traditionally, residents of Sechelt had purchased their clothing from Bert Whit-

88

aker's various general stores on the Boulevard, and later from the Union store. The first specialty shop selling men's garments was operated by "Deke" Deacon in the Village Centre complex on the south side of Cowrie west of Inlet Avenue. This building was erected in 1948 by Jim Parker and Captain P. McIntyre, who did business as Village Enterprises. The centre included the Village Coffee Shop (Jack Richardson), Ken Whitaker's insurance and real estate office, Lang's Rexall Drugs, the telephone office, Parker's Hardware, Sechelt Taxi and the Bank of Montreal's first office in Sechelt. "Deke" Deacon's men's clothing shop was taken over by Eva Lyons, who in turn sold the business to Joan Hansen. Joan specialized in women's wear, so Morgan Thompson purchased her stock of men's apparel. After moving to Cowrie Street, Morgan and Bill rented a tiny grocery store building which E.S. Clayton had opened in 1950 and vacated in 1956

when he and his family erected a larger store next door on Cowrie Street, at the east side of Trail Avenue. Morgan remained in the Clayton premises until 1961.

The name "Sechelt Men's Wear" was changed to "Morgan's Men's Wear" when Morgan Thompson purchased Bill Parson's share of the business in the early 1960s. By the time Bill died in 1977 he had become well known for the quality of his race horses, especially Hunechin Princess. He had operated a motel near the beach at Mission Point as well as Peninsula Logging Supply and a building supply store on Wharf Road. Dorothy and Bill also owned a farm on Mason Road.

While Morgan was using the Clayton premises his other neighbours on the south side of Cowrie included the Holy Family Church, Magistrate Andy Johnston's office and the police station, Chris's Variety Store (operated by Chris-

Cowrie Street, Sechelt, about 1946. The delivery truck is parked in front of the two-storey Sechelt Service Store, operated by Jack and Lee Redman. They purchased it from Joe Spangler on October 31, 1946, when it was the only store on the "back road." The building in the centre was the original Shell service station and Rockwood Lodge can be seen where Cowrie meets Shorncliffe Avenue. The fence on the right enclosed the house built by Jack Wood, telegrapher, and his wife Edythe, on ground now occupied by the dock.

tine Johnston, first mayor of Sechelt), George Philip's cottage, H.B. Gordon's office and the Village Centre complex.

On the north side of Cowrie in the period 1957 to 1961 Morgan's neighbours included the Shell station operated by Frank Solnik, Chrissie Crucil's Tasella Shop, the Gus Crucil home, Redman's Red and White Store, Ted Osborne's home, Dolly Dunn's house and the residence of Jack and Carrie Mayne.

In 1961 Morgan's Men's Wear moved into the premises then owned by Kurluk's Electric. In the spring of 1954, the year Morgan arrived in Sechelt, C & S Sales and Kurluk's Electric were clearing the trees from their building lot on the north side of Cowrie, bordering the east side of Inlet Avenue. Dan Currie recalled that he paid $40 per month for the land to the Union company through its resident agent, Ernie Parr Pearson. Dan Currie, Bill Swain and Ted Kurluk together put up a building sixty feet by fifty-five feet. William Swain was mayor of Sechelt in 1969–1971 and his daughter Doreen was the wife of Dan Currie.

The Kurluk premises on the eastern side of the building contained two small shops, each about thirteen feet wide. At a later period Helen Bishop operated a ladies' wear store in the thirteen feet next to C & S Hardware, while Morgan moved into the other thirteen feet. He purchased the building from Ted Kurluk about 1969 and expanded his business into the entire space.

Mr. Currie recalled that the land across on the north side of Cowrie had been Jack Nelson's used car lot. Whitaker House had stood at Cowrie and Inlet since 1907 and was still a private residence in 1954. East of the home there was once a popular tennis court and west of Whitaker House the Sechelt Volunteer Fire Brigade had a rough shack sitting right on the Inlet avenue road allowance.

For years before Inlet and Trail Avenues were opened up to the waterfront people reached the Boulevard from "the

Union Steamship Company employees in the early 1940s. Back row, left to right: James "Jimmy" Mowatt, storekeeper; unknown; Edric Clayton, store manager; Marjorie Hackett; Bert Hackett, Superintendent; Bill Edgar, butcher; "Bobby" Kean. Front row, left to right: Mrs. Bertram, hotel employee; Harry Billingsley, store clerk and butcher; Alex Kean, truck driver; Irene Wheeler, store and tea room clerk; Ken E. Wood, store clerk.

Sechelt's first gas station, standing at the northeast corner of Inlet Avenue and Cowrie Street.

back road" (as Cowrie was popularly known) by walking on a narrow plank sidewalk over the snake-infested bog behind the berm along Trail Bay. Contemporary developers have almost obliterated this marshy area with sand and gravel fill, but in the early 1950s it was still possible to harvest cranberries and bulrushes there. Visitors used to take cranberries from Sechelt back to Vancouver for canning. Yesterday's children loved the bog but today's will not realize that it ever existed.

In 1954 Village Enterprises put up its second building. Early tenants in the complex included the post office, the Bank of Montreal, Gladys Bachelor's beauty parlour and a doctor's office. When the Village of Sechelt was incorporated in February 1956 the first municipal office was also located in this building.

JACK AND LEE REDMAN'S STORES

IN 1946, COWRIE STREET was a dirt road with only one shop — the Sechelt Service Store — located between Inlet and Trail Avenues. On November 1 of that year Jack Redman and his uncle, Stuart Killick, took over the store from Joe Spangler and soon the men became so busy that Lee Redman and Nellie Killick worked to help them. They carried on a general business, selling not only groceries and meat, but also clothing and hardware such as axes and hot-air stoves. Later, as specialty shops opened in Sechelt, the Sechelt Service Store phased out the overlapping stocks and concentrated on groceries.

Putting up a customer's order back in 1946 was very different from today's routines. Ration cards introduced during the war were still required for the purchase of such items as sugar, tea, meat, butter and jello. There was no self-service at first. Each customer's requirements were written down in detail before the desired articles were assembled by the clerk. Freight for the store arrived via the Union Steamship boats which sailed from Vancouver three times a week: Tuesdays, 91

The south side of Cowrie Street, 1964.

Thursdays and Saturdays. Mr. Redman remembers waiting many weary hours for the boats to be unloaded so that he could truck supplies back to the shop where his customers were waiting for fresh bread and other groceries.

The store provided service seven days a week because logging camp orders were often received by radio telephone and shipped on Sundays when the men returned to camp. Also on Sundays Mr. and Mrs. Redman opened the store from one to three o'clock to accommodate the children from the residential school who came to buy their treats for the week.

Mr. Killick, a First World War veteran, retired about 1948 and Mr. Redman took over sole ownership under the name Sechelt Service Store. The business progressed well, serving an area from West Sechelt to Roberts Creek and providing free delivery. A decision was made to set up self-service, so counters were cut out, buggies acquired and a check-out installed.

To further reduce the congestion at the

Cowrie Street between Inlet and Trail Avenues, Christmas 1966.

Sechelt location Mr. Redman took over the Selma Park Store, which had been operated by Mr. and Mrs. Hubbs until about 1960. New fixtures and refrigeration were installed and the premises were stocked with meat and other groceries from the Sechelt store. Lee Redman ran the cash register and check-out while Dorothy Hubbs ran the post office and

92

helped in the store. The response was good and a fairly large business developed. Ken Wood bought out the Selma Park store after the Sechelt operation moved to more spacious quarters in 1963.

It was on November 20, 1963 that the Redman family opened for business on the ground floor of the new Lang Block, built on Cowrie Street by Ben Lang. Eventually the name of the business was changed to Redman's Red and White Market. The supplier was changed from Malkin to Kelly Douglas. The staff increased from two men in 1946 to five, and then to ten or twelve employees in the new building. Many local students who applied to Mr. Redman for after-school or summer work remembered with appreciation the training they received from him.

NORMAN WATSON'S STORES AND BUSINESSES

NORM WATSON and Frank Parker—who both arrived in Sechelt in the early 1950s and who both later became aldermen—had become partners in Sechelt Lockers by 1956. Their slogan was "No. 1 on the phone—No. 1 in the home." This was in the days when all telephone calls were placed through an operator stationed in the Village Centre building on Cowrie Street.

Sechelt Lockers' promotion in 1956 read: "Wholesale and retail fresh and frozen meats, fruits and vegetables. Peter's ice cream. Rent a locker & save under our new food plan." A front quarter of beef cost twenty-six cents per pound. Home freezers were not common at the time, so people rented Lockers in the firm's premises on Wharf Road.

In March 1957 Sechelt Lockers advertised "Herring bait in all sizes now in! New pack." This led Norm Watson and Frank Parker to establish the Tyee Bait Company in Sechelt. By 1958 the partnership was said to be the largest herring bait exporter in Canada. The Company

was probably the only industry within the village of Sechelt and provided employment for many Indian people. Tyee Bait became Tyee Products about 1970 and still does business in Sechelt, although under different ownership.

OTHER SERVICES

THE FIRST TAXI SERVICE in Sechelt was started around 1930 by Frank French and his wife Alice, and for some time this was the only taxi in Sechelt. Frank also opened Sechelt's first gas station at this time. The gas was hand pumped and Jack Nelson, who at one time leased the station from Frank French and later opened his own garage, stated that he once pumped 580 gallons of gas in one day. When Jack opened his own station on August 8, 1951, it featured the first electric gas pumps in Sechelt, dispensing gas at thirty cents per gallon. This gas station was located at the corner of Wharf Road and the highway.

A Standard Motor station was opened on October 31, 1953, and in 1955 Ernie Barker and Mickey Coe opened a pool hall above it. In July of 1957 Cliff Connor opened "Cliff's Shell Service," after taking over the station from Frank Solnik, and in 1961 Shell Oil spent $25,000 revamping the station at the corner of Cowrie and Trail, on the site of Frank French's first garage.

In the 1920s Joe Martin operated a bus service in Sechelt. He used to drive this "bus" onto the Sechelt wharf and pick up passengers from the Union boats. The vehicle was not actually a bus, but rather an open truck into which benches had been placed for passengers to sit on. Privileged ladies occasionally sat with the driver. The passengers' luggage was fitted around their feet. The vehicle Joe drove was known as the "Flying Goose" because it had black tarpaulins attached to the sides near the roof and these curtains flapped like wings as Joe drove along the deeply rutted roads of Sechelt. Dust rose behind any vehicle those days, forcing

The Coast News

PUBLISHED EVERY WEDNESDAY at HALFMOON BAY, B. C.

SERVING A PROGRESSIVE AND GROWING AREA ON BRITISH COLUMBIA'S SOUTHERN COAST, Including—

Irvine's Landing - Egmont - Hardy Island - Halfmoon Bay   Sechelt - Wilson Creek - Roberts Creek - Grantham's Landing

Gibson's Landing - Port Mellon - Hopkin's Landing - Secret Cove - Hillside

VOL. I, No. 2   Wednesday, July 16th, 1945   FIVE CENTS PER COPY. $2.50 PER YEAR, BY MAIL

Scholarship Offered To Papertown Students

DETAILS of the qualifications for the scholarship recently offered by Local 312 of the Pulp, Sulphite and Paper Mill Workers' Union at Ocean Falls have been made public by the committee in charge. The scholarship, to be known as the "Local 312 Award", applies to university entrance students in the five paper mill towns in the province—Powell River, Port Alice, Port Mellon, Woodfibre and Ocean Falls—and is based on the regulation scholarship exams as required by the University of British Columbia or the Department of Education.

The scholarship will entitle the winner to first-year tuition fees in any university, or to the taking of a trade-school, business or home-training course. It has a maximum value of $200. The recipient of the award is eligible for its full benefits at any time within a period of 5 years from the date of award.

The courses are, however, subject to the approval of the Local 312 Committee in charge of the award, and subject to proof of entering and conscientiously carrying out the studies.

ROBERTS CREEK . . .

School Problem Is Discussed

A meeting of ratepayers was held at the home of Mrs. Haslam, to discuss the school situation in Roberts Creek. The construction of a three-room elementary school at Roberts Creek and the amalgamation of Elphinstone Bay School District with the Gibson United School District were the main topics of the evening.

Dominion Government regulations banning conventions has caused postponement of the annual meeting of the B.C. Credit Union League, which was to have been held June 29th and 30th in the Hotel Vancouver. Tentative dates have been set for August 24th and 25th, when the convention will be held if regulations permit. It is hoped that everyone interested will attend.

We Apologize! We Think Gibson's Is One Of The Best!

In spite of getting off to a bit of a bad start with our friends at Gibson's by leaving that town off our masthead last week, we managed to draw one bouquet out of the maelstrom.

From Russ Gatzke, at Gibson's, came this encouraging note: "I must say that I like your paper very much and believe it should be a big help to everybody."

ROBERTS CREEK . . .

FO. Mathews And PO. Farrar Home

Flying-Officer J. O. Mathews is spending a leave at Roberts Creek with his mother, Mrs. J. Mathews. Johnny has spent a year and a half overseas with the RCAF, partly on Transport Command. He has made four flights across the Atlantic.

Petty-Officer L. H. Farrar is home on leave with his mother, Mrs. Frances Farrar of Roberts Creek. PO Farrar is a member of the RCN, and has three more years to serve. He was with the Channel striking force.

PORT MELLON . . .

New Townsite Work Progresses Rapidly

The new townsite program at Port Mellon is progressing very rapidly. The clearing and levelling of the grounds should be completed in a few days. The work also includes the new school recreation grounds.

Capt. F. Dredge, of the Pacific Coast Militia Rangers and the ARP at Gambier Harbor, paid an official visit to Port Mellon early in July.

Miss Mildren Graham, formerly of Chilliwack, has taken over the duties of Assistant Postmaster at Port Mellon, relieving Miss Frances Macklin. Miss Graham has had considerable experience in the postal department, having worked in Chilliwack and Vancouver.

Mrs. Gordon McKenzie and son have left for the East on an extended visit with her parents.

Mr. and Mrs. Royal Smith of Middletown, Ohio, arrived on July 7 for a week's holidays. Mr. Smith is on the engineering staff of the Sorg Paper Co.

Mr. and Mrs. Arthur Francis and daughter, of Vancouver, spent a week-end visiting in Port Mellon recently. Mr. Francis was formerly chief engineer for the Sorg Pulp Co.

Mr. Louis Biden, master mechanic for Sorg Pulp Co., has left their employ and has returned to Vancouver. Mr. Jim Veitch is also leaving the Sorg employ and intends to take up residence at Gibson's Landing.

Mr. Harry Taylor, recently of Ocean Falls, has taken over the duties as head of the pipe-fitting department.

Dredging operations have begun on Sorg's new program to make storage room for Cariboo pulpwood.

Unusual Souvenir . . .

Travellers in the Sechelt Inlet will recognize the Wilson home in the accompanying sketch. During a holiday visit with Mr. and Mrs. D. Wilson a friend, Miss Phyllis Laycock, made a sketch of the residence and surroundings and made a tapestry in full color of the wonderful view. The framed picture is a work of art, finished in detail and, naturally, treasured greatly by Mr. and Mrs. Wilson.

HALFMOON BAY . . .

SUMMER BRINGS HOLIDAYERS TO HALFMOON BAY

Mr. and Mrs. V. S. Osborne and daughter Shirley, of Westview, have returned here for a short time to visit old friends. Vic Osborne is in charge of the logging trucks of the Osborne Lumber and Mercantile Co, which are hauling logs for the Alaska Pine Co. at Powell River.

Miss Laverne Anderson is spending her summer holidays with her mother and step-father, Mr. and Mrs. W. Kalterman.

Mrs. Clarence Moorhouse and infant daughter arrived from Mission recently to reside at Narrows Arm, where Mr. Moorhouse is employed by the Osborne Logging Co. They made their first home here about seven years ago, and about a year later Moorhouse left to go to Persia, where he was employed in the oil fields by the Standard Oil Co. Mrs. Moorhouse joined him there later. They lived in Persia several years, but returned to Canada due to conditions there after the war broke out.

Mr. and Mrs. R. P. Mullen are visiting friends and relatives in Vancouver for a brief period.

Elmer McDonald is leaving for the prairies shortly. It is his intention to stay there for several months, and he will most likely take a part in the harvesting. His wife and young daughter will visit her parents, Mr. and Mrs. Berdahl, at Gibson's Landing while he is away.

Mr. and Mrs. Bert Harding and children spent a week visiting Mrs. Harding's parents, Mr. and Mrs. Westbrook, at Hardy Island.

FOREST BAN IS LIFTED MONDAY

CLOSURE of coast forests, in effect for the past week after high temperatures and low humidity made the fire menace highly acute, was lifted at noon Monday, forestry officials informed the Coast News.

The release of the ban will allow resumption of logging operations, as well as letting fishermen and berry-pickers into the woods.

The officials warn, however, that the district had only a light rain "in spots," and that people in the bush should be very careful with fire. No blazes of any consequence have broken out in the peninsula area so far this year, though Vancouver Island experienced some of its most disastrous outbreaks since the great Campbell River conflagration of 1938.

9000 Feet of Water Main Put In At Gibson's

ADDITIONAL PIPES WILL ENABLE MANY MORE USERS TO BE SERVED

PORT MELLON . . .

Ray Nourice Passes in Vancouver

Mr. Ray Nourice, proprietor of the Seaside Hotel for several years, passed way in the Vancouver General Hospital on Tuesday, July 3rd.

Mr. Nourice is mourned by many people in this district. He leaves his wife and one son, who is in the Royal Air Force and arrived home just in time to be with his father before he passed away.

Funeral services were held from Nunn & Thomson's Chapel.

Mr. George T. Klein has returned from his holiday trip to Toronto and district, and is now working with Mr. Downes.

Miss Clara Knowles of West Vancouver is spending a week with Mrs. Farrar of Roberts Creek.

FO R. F. Hughes, DFM, is home on leave prior to leaving for the Pacific theatre. Ronnie spent two and a half years overseas with the RAF and RCAF. He made 31 flights over Germany. Ronnie was formerly employed by the B&K Logging Co. at Elk Bay and Roberts Creek.

SECHELT . . .

The Women's Auxiliary of the Canadian Legion are having their annual tea and summer sale on July 26th in the Legion Hall.

The first issue of the "Coast News" is being distributed at Gibson's Landing. Residents note, with appropriate humility, that this district is not among those intended to be served by the new venture, according to the published prospectus.

The Village of Gibson's Landing has just completed laying about 9,000 feet of water supply main, bringing water from springs near the foot of the mountain to the reservoir to augment the pumped supply. The supply now available makes it possible to provide water to the Howe Sound United School, and to some of the residents outside the village who have been badly in need of water for many years. The rapidly increasing demand for water service within the village must also be provided for.

The Howe Sound United School is now engaged in the installation of sanitary facilities and drinking fountains, made possible through the new water supply. This has been an urgent need for several years.

The Howe Sound Transport (Ballentine and Frith) expect to be able to commence operation of a ferry service to Horseshoe Bay about August 1st.

SMALLER JAM PACK

Jam-making at the plant of the Howe Sound Co-operative Canning Association commenced during the latter part of June. The pack of strawberry jam promises to be low, but the raspberry jam should be considerably above last year.

pedestrians to close their eyes and mask their mouths with their hands when a car went by. To get a ride to the wharf one simply stood beside the road with one's luggage—telephones were extremely rare in private homes. The fare depended on the distance carried and there were no tickets.

Joe would also deliver vegetables, fruits and firewood in his bus, but this service was more often provided in Sechelt by Jack Reeves of Roberts Creek, who made his rounds in a horse-drawn wagon.

PROFESSIONAL SERVICES

THE FIRST DOCTOR IN SECHELT was Arnold Holm, who came to the town in 1939. He stayed initially in Jack Mayne's house, then he located in a cottage on the waterfront before setting up an office on Cowrie Street. Dr. Holm also served as the community's first coroner. Dr. Hugh Inglis of Gibsons also offered medical counsel, serving residents as far up as Halfmoon Bay. Dr. Duncan McColl arrived in Sechelt in the years following World War II.

The law firm of Hutchison, Maitland and Legg from Vancouver started an office in Sechelt on April 16, 1955, and were represented in town by Robert Maitland.

The *Coast News* was the first newspaper based in Sechelt. It was started by Al Alsgard and Ernie Parr Pearson, and its first issue came out on July 11, 1945. The paper moved to Gibsons in 1949. A previous newspaper, the *Red, White and Blue*, was initiated in 1939 by Gordon Head, Don King and Ted Osborne and operated for a brief time out of Halfmoon Bay. Other early newspapers serving the Sunshine Coast included the *Eagle*, a small folded sheet initiated in 1931 out of Gibsons, the *Independent* in Roberts Creek and the *Peninsula Times*, which was run by Claude Hoodspith of West Vancouver.

PUBLIC
UTILITIES,
INSTITUTIONS
AND
BUILDINGS

RPH

UTILITIES
Electricity

MANY EARLY SETTLERS obtained heat from wood-burning stoves and light from lamps that burned white gas or kerosene. There were some early settlers, though, who had their own generators for obtaining electric power. Charles Jordan, who lived on the east bank of Cook Creek, installed a dam in the stream to provide electricity for his home. Sarah and Tom Wall, who located in Halfmoon Bay in about 1919, had a pelton wheel near their home to supply electricity, as did the Indian reserve. Florence Cliff Montgomery remembered Duncan Irvine having a light plant powered by a waterfall and he had so much electricity that he could lie in bed, press buttons, and the chicken house door would open, or lights would go on. Opeongo Lodge, which was ready for occupancy by 1926, had a gas-powered Delco generator. In the living room of the lodge, the bare light bulbs were covered by inverted parasols.

Most communication was conducted by telegraph, which was established in Sechelt in 1913. Charles Bradbury was the first telegraph officer. By 1921 a telephone line had been put in place that ran from Sechelt through Gibsons and beyond Port Mellon up Howe Sound. There were two telephones in Sechelt in those days, one owned by Bert Whitaker in the general store and one at the Sechelt Indian school.

In 1936 the Columbia Power Company began a project to supply power to the lower part of the Sunshine Coast. The line started at a diesel electric station at Selma Park, and extended to Gibsons. By 1937 or 1938, public electric power was available to residents of Sechelt. According to Frank Wyngaert, "the acceptance of this service was extremely slow. We were in mid-depression years. Few people indeed could afford to have their home wired to receive the service." The service was initially used by approximately fifty people.

In 1945 the BC Power Commission took over from the Columbia Power Company, and in the late spring of 1952 a power station was established at Clowhom Falls, and a twenty-two-mile transmission line was extended to

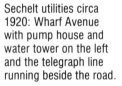

Sechelt utilities circa 1920: Wharf Avenue with pump house and water tower on the left and the telegraph line running beside the road.

Sechelt. The diesel electric station at Selma Park was closed at this time. BC Electric superseded the BC Power Commission in 1955. On November 23, 1956 the first twenty-three street lights in Sechelt were turned on. The Clowhom station was expanded in 1957, and a sub-station was constructed at Sechelt in the same year. In 1962 the BC Power Commission and BC Electric were merged under the umbrella of BC Hydro, and in 1968 a new high-voltage line was put in place between Cheekeye, near Squamish, and Sechelt.

The BC Telephone Company took over telephone services from the federal government in the early 1950s and announced in 1954 that it would bring the system up to date. In 1959 a $850,000 expansion program was undertaken by BC Telephone and by 1961 there were 687 phones at Sechelt and 2,183 between Port Mellon and Pender Harbour.

Water

AS WITH ELECTRICITY, many of the early residents of Sechelt obtained water from their own private sources. T. J. Cook initially got his water from a spring up the hill behind St. Hilda's Church. He brought the water down as far as his house in a pipe, and there were outdoor taps near his front steps. He left the tap running in cold weather to avoid having the pipes freeze — a common problem in the winters — but once when he was away someone turned the tap off and the pipes froze and cracked. After that he dug a well and installed a pump.

Some settlers applied to the Water Rights Branch of the Department of Lands of BC to divert water to use on

Charles Bradbury, Sechelt's first telegraph operator, and whose many photographs provide a valuable visual record of early Sechelt.

their own property. Charles Jordan applied for a permit to take water from Cook Creek, and in March 1923 was granted five hundred gallons per day for domestic use and five thousand gallons per day to power his hydraulic dam. In October 1925 Abe Mason was granted an allowance to take one hundred gallons

Sechelt's water supply transported from Chapman Creek in 1966.

98

Children getting some water from an outdoor tap on Sechelt Reserve No. 2 in the 1930s. As early as the late 1800s, water was carried to the Indian lands from higher elevations by flumes. The same water system was initially used by Bert Whitaker for his businesses, and was gathered in a water tower on the Whitaker property.

"GETTING A DRINK FOR SISTER," INDIAN CHILDREN SECHELT. B.C 593. H. McCALL, PHOTO,

per day for domestic use and one thousand gallons per day for additional power.

A reservoir system was developed by the Indian Band around 1889 or 1890. The water was brought down from what may have been Chapman (Mission) Creek in a flume and stored in a reservoir on the reserve. Around 1900 the Sechelt Band replaced the first flume with another, and in addition to serving their own needs this flume carried water down to a water tower just west of Wharf Road near the ocean front. Bert Whitaker used this water in the summer for his hotel and store. He also used a windmill-driven pump located west of Wharf Road. The Union Company established a flume that ran along a similar path to the Indian reserve, and for many years provided water to the community. A well at Selma Park provided water for the community there.

SECHELT POST OFFICE

IT WAS ON MARCH 1, 1896, that Sechelt's first post office was officially established. There had been, however, mail service of a sort prior to that time. The following

The original post office, seen here in 1904, was located on the Boulevard with the trail to Porpoise Bay (now Wharf Avenue) running between it and the barn to its right. Observe "Post Office" printed above the open doorway and a mail slot on its left, with a rain barrel and peavey at the corner. Whitaker operated a store in the same premises, which he had taken over from an earlier resident. When he built a new two-storey post office and store in 1899 the pioneer structure was used again as a bunkhouse, which had been its original purpose when built around 1890 (Alfred Whitaker and four of his sons lived in it for a time). People in the photo include Frank Strachan, a visitor from Vancouver, seated on the barrel, Jack Vickers, a beachcomber, standing in the doorway, and Pete LeVesque, and employee of Bert Whitaker's, holding the horse on the right.

The interior of Bert Whitaker's fourth store and post office in the building he erected in 1915 or 1916 on the Boulevard west of Wharf Road, probably during the 1920s. Mail was sorted into pigeon holes on the post office wall. When the sorting was completed the top of the dutch door was opened to serve the queue of people waiting. There were no mail boxes at this time.

excerpt from the *News Advertiser* dated January 3, 1894 gives an account of the route taken weekly by the Union Steamship Company vessel *Comox* after she made her first stop at Gibsons en route to Port Neville:

The next stopping place is Sechelt, where a number of settlers are now located. On Porpoise Bay, a short distance at the back of the Indian Mission, several more have taken up land and now that the settlement has increased so largely it is the intention to ask the postal authorities to establish a post office at Sechelt.

After a short run, Welcome Pass

is reached. Here a Post Office has recently been opened. The mail for Sechelt settlers is left here, but though not very far distant, it is often inconvenient to go for the mail.

Before postal money orders were sold locally, the crews of the steamers were generous enough to purchase these items in Vancouver for the settlers. T.J. Cook lived near the beach on property that was not far west of Snickett Park. He used to row out to the *Comox* to collect mail, and other settlers would call at his cabin to pick up their letters. It is possible that Mr. Cook was not an official postmaster, but he performed the service for his and a few scattered neighbours' convenience. (A story about him in the *Vancouver Sun Magazine Supplement* of December 11, 1954, when he was still living, states that in 1895 "–he became the first postmaster for the district—a service for which he received $20 a month. There was no wharf at Sechelt at the time, and he had to row out to meet the mail boat twice a week." The present Canada Post Office district authority has no knowledge of Mr. Cook's service, but says that its records may not be complete.)It is official, however, that Herbert Whitaker was appointed postmaster effective March 1, 1896 and that he continued until April 3, 1914. In the years around 1910 the ships in his Sechelt Steamship Company carried the mail between Vancouver and Sechelt. He also owned small boats running up Sechelt Inlet, and Joe Gregson recalled that Mr. Whitaker transported mail to the logging camps up the inlet early in the century and charged each man twenty-five cents per month for the service.

Following the locations of the Sechelt post office during the Whitaker years can be a confusing task, as it was moved regularly according to where there was room for it. The first home of the post office was a one-story shingled shack with a lean-to on either side. Bert Whita- 101

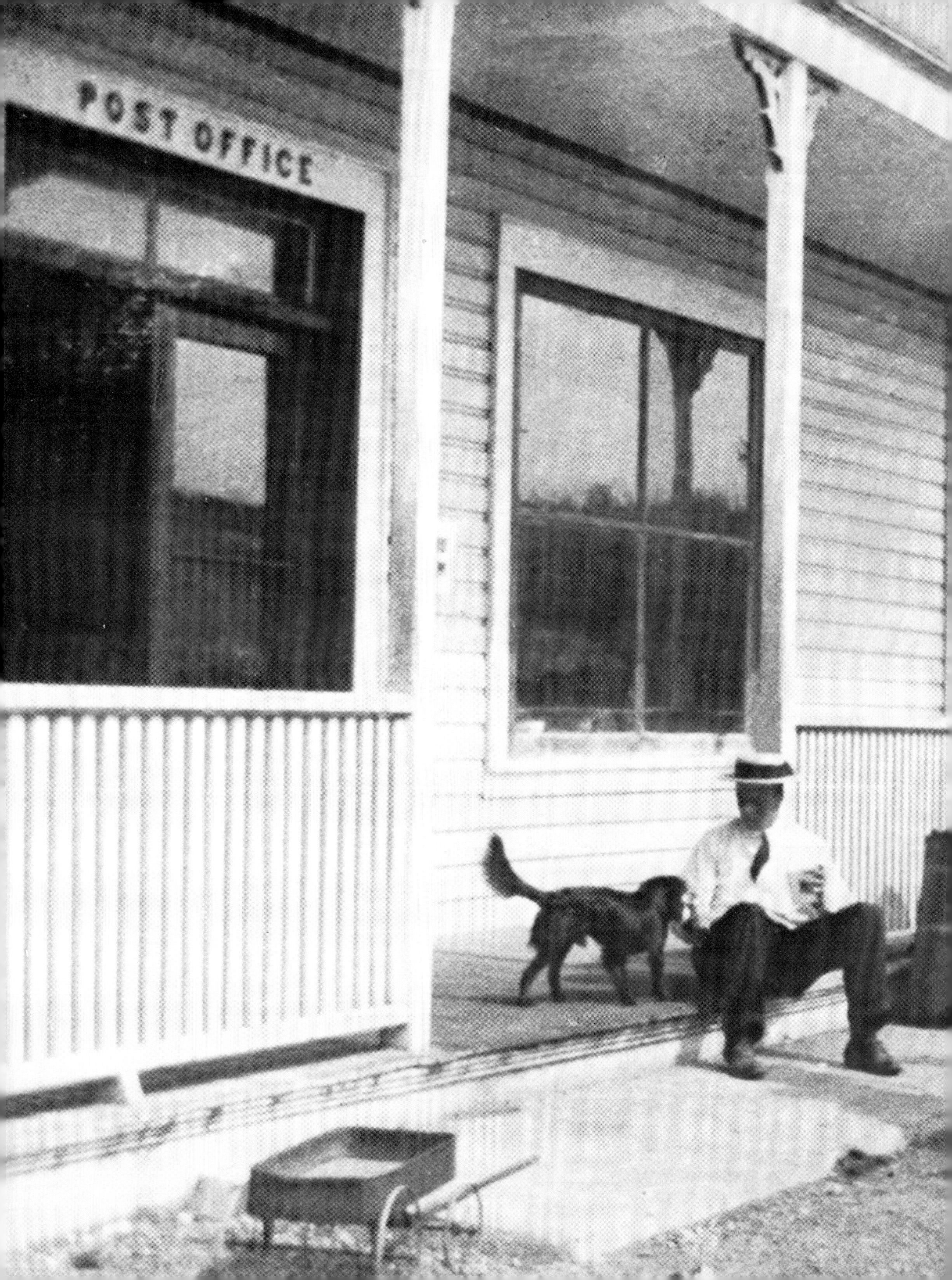
POST OFFICE

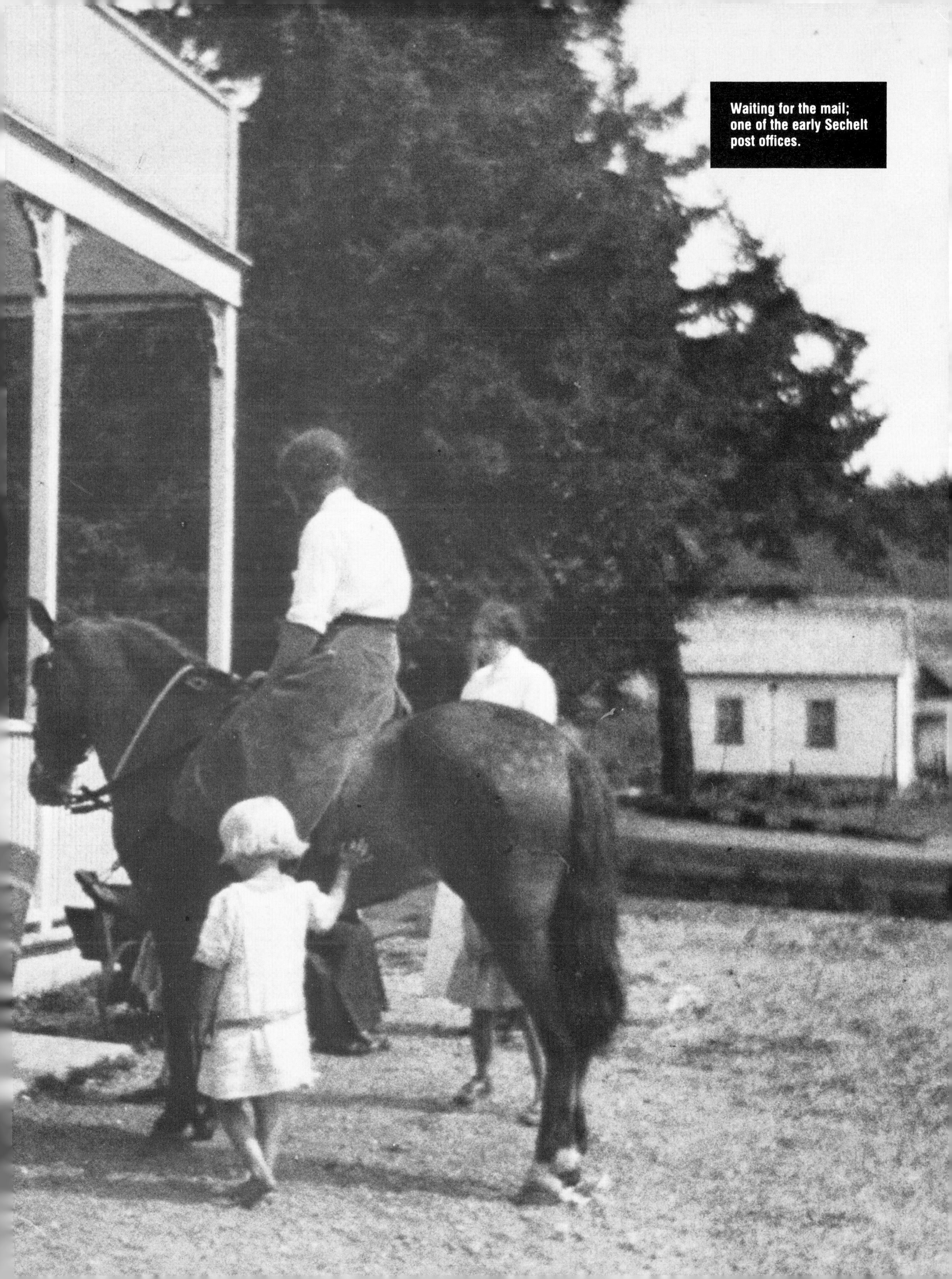

Waiting for the mail; one of the early Sechelt post offices.

Postmaster Robert Hackett, (back row centre) presides over a 1950 post office ceremony. The Brownies were given prints of stagecoaches.

ker built it as his first store at Trail Bay. It was also used as a stopping place and was located on the Boulevard at the end of what is today Wharf Road. The second post office building also served at various times as Mr. Whitaker's second store, the first telegraph office and the first school outside the Indian village. The third location of the Sechelt post office was in a building which had also served as Mr. Whitaker's third store and an annex to his first hotel. It was converted entirely into a hotel when the first one burned down. This store-hotel building was erected about 1907 and destroyed by fire on July 22, 1937. The Petro- Canada oil tanks are now standing in the proximity of the old site.

After the first hotel burned down in 1914, another general store (Mr. Whitaker's fourth) was built on the seafront bordering the west side of Wharf Road. This building became the fourth home of the post office and remained so until the end of 1954. It was a two-storied wooden building, the top floor being used, like Whitaker's previous store, as a hotel annex. This store was later oper-

ated by the Union Steamship Company.

The second postmaster, Thomas P. O'Kelly, was appointed for a short period from May 1 to October 8, 1914. He was a partner of Mr. Whitaker's for a brief time. Mr. George J. Stockman was appointed postmaster on December 1, 1914 and served until November 18, 1915.

Bert Whitaker, who sold out all his interests to Baron von Lutwitz, a German, in 1913, retrieved the holdings after the outbreak of the First World War and was reappointed postmaster, holding the post from January 1, 1916 until November 22, 1925. He was succeeded by his friend, George H.R. Aman, from February 2, 1926 to May 14, 1928. Robert S. Hackett, who had been acting postmaster after Mr. Aman, was postmaster from September 7, 1928 until 1950. Belinda A. Gaines was appointed postmistress on November 6, 1950.

Until May 29, 1950, mail bound for Sechelt travelled directly from Vancouver by water. Effective May 30, direct water service was replaced and mail service restructured as follows: (1) Land service between Vancouver and the wharf at Horseshoe Bay (2) Water service via Black Ball Ferries between the wharf at Horseshoe Bay and the wharf at Gibsons (3) Land service by the Sechelt Motor Transport Company from the wharf at Gibsons to the Sechelt Post Office.

Effective January 2, 1952 the above three services were replaced by a Highway Service operating between Vancouver and Halfmoon Bay via the Horseshoe Bay–Gibsons ferry calling en route at the Sechelt Post Office.

A lease was completed for January 1, 1955, whereby Village Enterprises (Jim E. Parker and Captain McIntyre) supplied premises on Cowrie Street which became the fifth home of the post office. These quarters were designed specifically to suit the requirements of the department. In the larger premises it became possible for the public to rent boxes in the lobby, which speeded up service. Ultimately, though, the Post Office was moved to its present location at the corner of Inlet Avenue and Dolphin Street.

In the pioneer days of Sechelt, going to the village on boat day to pick up letters, newspapers and gossip was a social occasion in the lives of isolated residents who had no telephones or radios and little in the way of transportation or even roads. They came to see who got off the boat — expected house guests, day-trippers, week-enders for the hotel and staff picnic parties. It was fun to watch the freight unloaded, everything from groceries and furniture through to boomchains and the occasional horse. Then there would be a long queue in front of the post office wicket while waiting for the mail to be sorted. Bystanders counted the mailbags as they were carried into the post office in order to form an estimate of how long the wait would be. Bets were placed on the duration of the time lapse. Children sent for the mail enjoyed the chore because they could chew toffee bars (purchased from the glass case on the store counter) until the top section of the post office door swung open as a signal that the mail was ready for distribution. The only drawback to the youngsters' expeditions was finding a route home which would avoid the many wild cows wandering at large, their bells tinkling as they grazed.

John and Clara Lyell prior to 1922.

Murder at Halfmoon Bay

CLARA LYELL was born in England in 1859 and before she married John Lyell was the wife of Charles Priestland, who applied to pre-empt District Lot 1638 at Halfmoon Bay on October 7, 1892, and after whom Priestland Cove is named.

The 1915 Sessional Papers of the Canadian Parliament give information on the local government telegraph service, stating that Mrs. Lyell was appointed agent at Welcome Pass on May 17, 1913, with remuneration consisting of a 25 percent commission. Wrigley's BC directory for 1918 uses the new name Halfmoon Bay and lists John Lyell, by then Clara's second husband, as postmaster.

Perhaps Mrs. Lyell's hair was flaxen in her youth, but as I remember her from my childhood the outstanding features of her appearance were her snow white hair and frail figure. She was a living legend and passengers on the Union Steamship vessels pointed her out to one another as they leaned against the ships' rails while she personally picked up the mail bag.

In 1922, Clara's husband John was suspected of murdering logger Bob Rainey. The *Vancouver Province* of July 17, 1922 described events as follows:

> Murder mystery at Half Moon Bay. Bullet kills R.W. Rainey—Police searching for suspect.
>
> Assisted by two bloodhounds, a posse is today searching the bush in the vicinity of Halfmoon Bay for the murderer of R.W. Rainey.
>
> His body was found Thursday about 100 yards from his house. A rifle bullet had entered from behind the left shoulder, penetrating the heart. The body was discovered by a dog and was hidden under brush, ferns and alder branches. It was brought to Vancouver last night on the steamer *Chilco*.
>
> Rainey was a young unmarried logger, employed by the Gordon Development Company.
>
> The bloodhounds are the same dogs used in the attempt to trace Mr. Harry B. Jackson, missing Hotel Vancouver manager.
>
> Information from Halfmoon Bay is to the effect that a man whom the police suspect committed the crime, has taken to the woods. He is armed with a rifle. The bush in the locality is very thick and bloodhounds were requisitioned to pick up the scent.
>
> A posse has been organized by Chief Cruikshanks of the Provincial Police, Vancouver. He is assisted by Constable Hadley of Powell River and Game Warden Kearns of Pender Harbour.

The mystery remained unsolved and John Lyell was never found or brought to trial. One explanation offered in later years is that he escaped the bloodhounds by walking through the water breaking on the beach to throw the dogs off his scent and subsequently worked his passage to Australia.

POLICING PIONEER SECHELT

IN APRIL 1915 T.J. Cook became the first resident magistrate in Sechelt when he was appointed a justice of the peace for the province of BC. This was years before there was a resident policeman or government office of any kind in Sechelt, so people from the surrounding area brought their practical as well as legal problems to Mr. Cook. He helped with matters ranging from how to treat a sick dog to the organization of neighbours to check on isolated residents after a bad wind storm. He administered the Oath of Allegiance to many settlers seeking Canadian citizenship, including Abe Mason.

Frank French was appointed the first Provincial Police constable in Sechelt in 1919, and in 1927 T.D. Sutherland was appointed a probationary game constable with E Division of the Provincial Police. He was stationed at Sechelt, where he continued for a decade to serve the area as game warden. He was promoted to police corporal in 1937 and to sergeant in the Powell River District in 1938.

In the years before Sechelt had a policeman, charges would be made by the fisheries officer, the game warden, or even an offended neighbour or an abused wife. T.J. Cook held court in his own dining room, and as a small child I was free to wander in and out to hear whatever case might be under discussion. Game Warden Sutherland came often to lay charges or present evidence. What I chiefly remember about him in the 1920s is that he brought with him his huge, shaggy blonde dog, named Trotsky after the Russian revolutionary.

One of my grandfather's old journals

The little log cabin that once housed the police and relief office as it appeared in 1981.

Constable Tom B. Marsh of Pender Harbour in front of the Sechelt Police office in one of the orchard cottages in 1941.

includes an entry dated December 15, 1932, as follows: "Albert N... of Halfmoon Bay was charged by T.D. Sutherland, Game Warden, with unlawfully being in possession of a Willow Grouse during the close season. Pleading Guilty fined $10.00 with $1.50 Costs. Thomas J. Cook J.P." Crime in Sechelt in the early days was seldom more serious than this.

In another case I can remember an Indian was accused of a minor offence. My grandfather sentenced him to jail and told him to go home and cut enough firewood for his wife to last her the month he would be imprisoned. The next day the offender was instructed to board the Union boat to Vancouver and he would be met by a man known as the "Indian Policeman." In the case of a white offender, he would be met at the gangplank in Vancouver by a Provincial policeman. Sechelt acquired a telegraph operator (Charles Bradbury) in 1913, so my grandfather simply sent a wire to the police, asking them to meet the boat. There was never a problem of a prisoner running away.

T.J. Cook settled civic disputes as well. W.J. Martin recalled one such dispute: "I will never forget the evening Mrs. Gugin took my father to court for telling her to button her lip . . . Johnny Cook dismissed 107

the case and told them both to keep the peace."

A small log cabin opposite the Wakefield Inn—which was built in 1926 as the home of T.D. Sutherland and his wife—served in the 1930s as a combination police office and relief office. Betty Ingram, who was a clerk in the office, remembered that T.D. Sutherland's time was taken up mostly by the relief work. She recalled that the relief camps on the Sunshine Coast were run more or less directly from Vancouver or Victoria. One was located at Wood Bay, near the east side of Malaspina Strait. The men in the camps worked for about twenty cents per day, and were put to work making roads or hand-hewing cedar logs for culverts. As for police work, Betty Ingram recalls that T.D. Sutherland always put in an appearance at the Saturday night dances "'just in case,' but he was seldom required in a law enforcement capacity."

It has long been rumoured that the log cabin opposite the Wakefield Inn also served as Sechelt's first jail, but this is false. The first jail in Sechelt was established in 1939, when the police and relief departments vacated the log cabin office and rented one of the Union company's orchard cottages. A jail was set up in one of the bedrooms. The cell, recalled Betty Ingram, was quite primitive: "As to who had the honour of being its first overnight guest I cannot remember, but he had my sympathy."

The Wakefield Inn was sold in 1940 and was converted by Charles F. Reda into a beer parlour, while the log cabin languished until the 1950s, when it was the home of a succession of coffee shops. It still stands today, unoccupied and in a state of disrepair.

Jack Mayne became stipendiary magistrate in 1939 for an area stretching from Port Mellon to Lasqueti Island, and remained in the post for three years. In 1954 Mr. Mayne became a notary public in Sechelt. Andrew Johnston also served as a notary public and magistrate for fifteen years following the Second World War, and in April of 1975 Maureen Corbin, previously a clerk at Sechelt Provincial Court, became the first female justice of the peace on the Sunshine Coast.

Internment of the Sunshine Coast Japanese, 1942

ON DECEMBER 7, 1941 Japan attacked Pearl Harbour and was soon at war with both the United States and Canada. On February 26, 1942 the Mackenzie King government ordered the removal of all people of Japanese ancestry from a protected area a hundred miles wide along the BC coast.

The Sunshine Coast had been for many years a beloved home to families of Japanese Canadians, some of them naturalized citizens, who established themselves in such occupations as fishing, logging, and agriculture. In spite of this, though, wartime brought a great deal of popular suspicion to bear on the Japanese community. An example is a *Coast News* report in 1945 which stated that "a new species of seaweed along the coast is regarded as an act of wartime sabotage by the Japanese boat owners and commercial fishermen."

After the removal edict under the War Measures Act time some time passed without anything happening. Then suddenly the police came for the local Japanese. They were ordered to be ready to board a Union Steamship vessel the next day. The Japanese fishermen and storekeepers at Egmont, such as Kay Hatashita and Ted Hyashi, who operated a floating store supplying the fishing community there, were told to be ready to go by 8 a.m., when they were taken to Pender Harbour to board the ship. The Konishi family, which for thirty years had operated a well-run farm on the west side of Porpoise Bay, boarded a vessel at Sechelt.

Two lines of fishboats confiscated from Japanese men being towed by fish packers into Pender Harbour in early 1942, after the outbreak of war between Japan and Canada in December 1941.

The evacuation was spread over the months from March to October 1942. During the first phase the Japanese from areas other than Vancouver were required on short notice to pack only the barest essentials and move hurriedly to a camp on the Exhibition grounds in Vancouver.

People who were told to take with them only what they could carry were confronted with the heart-breaking problem of hurriedly saying goodbye to almost every article they cherished. Some of the women sat down and wept as they chose what to pack. There was little opportunity to safeguard their property.

Our navy took charge of rounding up the Japanese fishboats. The boats from Sechelt Inlet, Egmont, Agamemnon Channel and other proximate areas were towed into Pender Harbour. Engine parts were removed so that the vessels would not run, then the navy assigned larger boats to tow the seized craft to the Fraser River. Some of the boats were very fine, but all were eventually sold by the Custodian of Enemy Alien Property for whatever they would fetch.

The Konishi farm at Porpoise Bay was purchased by a white man who failed to maintain it as a producing unit. During 1971 and 1972 a "hippy" commune established itself on a portion of the farm and attempted to grow food by organic methods. Old Jiro Konishi did more work by himself than this whole group achieved together.

During the second stage of the evacuation Japanese-Canadians went to various destinations in the interior of British Columbia, Ontario or the Prairies. Even though hostilities ended in 1945, the wartime restrictions continued until April, 1 1949. Until then no persons of Japanese descent could enter the coastal area without a permit. Most of the evacuees from the Sunshine Coast did not return because by that time they had established themselves elsewhere. Occasionally, however, the survivors still visit their former homes or send their dead back for burial on the Sechelt Peninsula.

SECHELT'S MUNICIPAL OFFICES

THE PLEBISCITE to decide whether Sechelt taxpayers wanted incorporation as a village municipality was held on January 21, 1956 following public meetings on the topic dating back as far as 1948. The population was estimated at 400, of whom 245 were adults. Voting day weather was miserable but the turnout was considered to be "wonderful." Ballots cast numbered 157, made up of 86 in favour and 71 against incorporation. On February 15, 1956 letters patent were issued in the name of Queen Elizabeth II, appointing a board of commissioners to govern Sechelt Municipality until an election could be held. This pro tem board consisted of Ted Osborne, Steve Howlett (acting chairman) and Ernie Parr Pearson. They set to work on February 21 by appointing Ralph Johnson as temporary village clerk-treasurer.

The First Office

THE INTERIM BOARD worked out of the incorporation committee rooms located on the upper floor of the two-storied Village Enterprises building, erected in 1954–55 for the late Jim Parker and Captain Perth McIntyre on the south side of Cowrie Street between Inlet Avenue and Wharf Road. The commissioners conducted their business around a table borrowed from the chamber of commerce.

The first election took place in the old Legion hall on April 14, 1956. At that time the physical boundaries of the municipality were much smaller than today, enclosing only 513 acres of land and 154 acres of water. There were 221 names on the voters' list and no less than eleven candidates competed for five seats. In contrast, apathy seems to run rampant now when good people have to be coaxed to run for office.

The First Elected Council

ON APRIL 17, 1956 the first elected council was sworn in at the village office by Magistrate Andy Johnston. The commissioners were Christine Johnston, Bernel Gordon, Captain Sam Dawe, Alex Lamb and Frank Parker. Mrs. Johnston received the most votes and became chairman of commissioners. She continued in this office through 1966, when she retired for reasons of health.

The elected council kept Ralph Johnson as clerk-treasurer at a salary of $175 per month. On December 31, 1956 he submitted to the corporation a report on municipal activities during the year. His essay was explicit, concise, readable and of general interest. It was so good that a local newspaper printed it in full.

The first elected council continued to use the office established by the temporary group, at the cost of $350 per month. The office was open for three half-days per week.

The Second Office

AT A COMMISSION MEETING on June 6, 1956 the Standard Oil Company requested council's permission to build a bulk storage plant in the village, and on the same day the British American Oil Company (forerunner of Gulf) was granted a permit to construct a petroleum pipeline from the plant on Wharf Road to connect with the Sechelt wharf at Trail Bay. The establishment of the oil tank farm made it possible for the village to acquire its second municipal office, because BA Oil accepted the village commission's tender to move an old building from the company's site to one where it would be used as a municipal hall. The only cost to the village was the cost of removal.

The old BA building was loaded onto a truck and moved from Wharf Road near the Boulevard to about the middle of a lot on Inlet Avenue at Mermaid Street, newly acquired by the village for $1,335.55. The current municipal office is located on the south end of the same property, but it is not the same building.

When the second office was moved in 1956 it was known to most people as the 111

Sechelt's first village council, left to right: Frank Parker, Captain Samuel Dawe, Alex Lamb, Christine Johnston, Ralph Johnson (clerk) and Hugh Bernel Gordon.

former Bank of Montreal, but old timers aware of its long history referred to the building as the "Flea Pit." It earned this name because far back in the century it housed transient workers and had consequently become loaded with fleas. Later it was spruced up and used as a home for Chinese cooks at the second Sechelt Hotel. During the 1930s it was a residence for young women who found summer employment at the hotel.

The Flea Pit originally stood just east of the hotel, facing the Boulevard close to the Indian reserve. The second Sechelt Hotel, erected for Bert Whitaker in 1905–06, was purchased by the Union Steamship Company in 1926 and was destroyed by fire in July 1936, but the Flea Pit was saved from the blaze in spite of its proximity to the three-storey building. Thereafter it was used for several purposes and was moved a short distance to face Wharf Road.

The telephone office was located in the Flea Pit until 1948, when the phone and telegraph staff moved into the Village Centre building on Cowrie Street. Then the Flea Pit housed the first Bank of Montreal office in Sechelt, from 1948 until the bank moved into new premises on the south side of Cowrie in 1955. When Gerry Gibbons of Porpoise Bay was a youth he used to light the fire in the Flea Pit to heat it on days when bank personnel arrived from Gibsons—initially only

on a part-time basis—to operate our first financial institution.

After the Flea Pit arrived on Inlet Avenue in late August 1956 it was renovated and permanent fixtures were installed at a cost of $2,425.77. At the end of the year the building was conservatively valued at $3,500. Furniture and equipment cost $871.28. The old name was no longer appropriate and the building became known as the "White House." The formal opening took place with due ceremony on November 24, 1956. Close to three hundred people watched the proceedings, causing Chairman Ritchey of the Gibsons Village Commission to express surprise at the large number of citizens participating. The young municipality did things with commendable grace and enthusiasm. Julie Anne Steele, great-granddaughter of Thomas John Cook, cut the ribbon symbolizing the opening of the second municipal office.

Geoffrey Whitaker, young grandson of Bert Whitaker, presented a 1902 oil

The "Flea Pit," nearing the end of its tether as municipal hall, in July 1966. The most notable feature of the building's architecture was the four square wooden pillars supporting the porch roof at the front of the structure. These four white posts are observable in photographs of the building from the time it was a staff shelter behind the hotel, through its career as a telephone office, a bank, a municipal office and finally a source of hamburgers and ice cream cones.

painting of Sechelt to the village on behalf of his family. This picture now hangs in the library. Ernie Pearson, master of ceremonies for the day, presented the commission with a gavel made by E.F. "Ted" Cooke, MBE. Magistrate Johnston donated a guest book, which was signed by surviving pioneers; they also entered the years in which they settled at Sechelt. Ada Dawe gave an album of photos of old Sechelt, now located in the library.

The second big event of the day occurred when Chairman Chris Johnston turned on power to Sechelt's first street lights, installed by BC Electric. Mrs. Johnston quoted appropriately from the Bible: "Let there be light." Citizens retired to the old Legion hall, where tea was served under the convenership of Doris Berry.

After a decade of use the Flea Pit became too cramped. Council erected a stucco replacement office and the wooden White House was vacated on September 24, 1966. Both the 1966 and the new 1967 councils debated what to do with the old Flea Pit, but in the end they permitted the historic structure to be lost to future generations.

Several alternative uses for the old hall were considered: rent it out; sell it; renovate it and offer the space to the newly created Sunshine Coast Regional District; or move it to Hackett Park for use as a museum. In January 1967 the village

commissioners were still awaiting the arrival of a museum expert from Victoria to study the suitability of the old hall. Arguments against preservation included the costs of moving, clearing the new site and building a foundation.

In April 1967 council decided to call for tenders to sell the structure, and Joe Benner's bid of three hundred dollars was accepted on condition that the hall be moved by May 15. The old municipal office was transported to lease land on Sechelt Indian Reserve No. 2, facing Highway 101, and became the front portion of John Petula's Peninsula Drive-in Restaurant. It suffered a fire on December 7, 1975 and was thereafter demolished.

So the circle was completed; from a residence for hotel cooks to a fast-food outlet. Where better could one find an example of the adaptive re-use of buildings?

The Third Office

THE COMMISSIONERS had a great deal on their plates in 1966. They purchased a lot as a site for the Centennial Library, they worked toward expansion of the village boundaries and they discussed pushing through the two unfinished blocks of old Teredo Street.

On June 1, Mr. Bourrie of the Vancouver firm of Bourrie and McLennan, general contractors, appeared before council

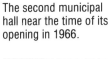

The second municipal hall near the time of its opening in 1966.

to discuss financial details and plans regarding the building of a two-storey municipal hall with a public office on the ground floor and a meeting chamber with further offices above. Mr. Bourrie had done similar work in Gibsons.

On July 6, 1966 the commissioners gave unanimous approval to erect a one-floor building of frame construction and stucco exterior finish, measuring 30.3 by 30.6 feet. This was said to be more than double the size of the old Flea Pit. The contract price of approximately $19,000 included the transfer as well as architect's fees, landscaping and complete finish.

The contract was let to the Vancouver firm without calling for tenders and this caused some ire. One letter to the editor complained as follows: "We are just now recovering from the shock of the new Sechelt Village Hall. The facts are being circulated so fast and furiously by word of mouth that there is no need to give the sordid details here of how seemingly sober local citizens would give an outsider the sum of $19,000 plus interest to build a $9,000 building. . ."Nonetheless, by the end of September the new office was occupied.

A Joint Facility

THE 1966 HALL was found to be smaller than citizens had anticipated. By the autumn of 1970 it was completely paid for and the council of the day immediately commenced planning for an extension in order to provide an adequate chamber with perhaps additional space for use as a courthouse. Early in 1971, however, a new council was in power and they opposed increasing the size.

The building sat in peace until April 1979, after which confusion reigned supreme for a long period. The school board and regional board met to discuss possible shared office space in Sechelt and the village was soon drawn into a tripartite project. The first plan was to move a portable school complex from Pender Harbour to the grounds of Chatelech School.

This proved unsuitable, and by May a new joint-use scheme had evolved in which the Village of Sechelt would provide the land and would trade the village office and site, together with the library and its two lots, for a plot on Shorncliffe Avenue opposite St. Hilda's Church. A public hearing, however, was required to rezone the property to public assembly. This was held July 1, 1979, when no less than five zoning amendments were discussed by a standing-room-only crowd of developers and residents. Participants called for a moratorium on all rezoning and made their displeasure known to council in no uncertain terms. The Ministry of Municipal Affairs decided to conduct a preliminary investigation into charges of irregularities in zoning, subdivision and development proposals in Sechelt.

Undaunted, council proceeded on July 31 to advertise notice of intention to sell the village office and library properties and buildings. They did indeed sell the municipal hall — conditional upon obtaining a suitable acre of land. At a meeting on February 4, 1981 council received a sizeable bill for legal fees incurred by the prospective purchaser a year and a half earlier.

By the end of August 1979 the developers had doubled the price of the proposed site for the joint-use facility on Shorncliffe Avenue and added a requirement that almost eight acres of their holdings be rezoned. Council ceased all discussion with them and proceeded to deliberate over eight other proposals made by a variety of developers.

Acting unilaterally, Sechelt council passed a resolution to purchase Lot 2, adjoining the Sechelt marsh. The regional board was concerned that it had not been consulted, that rezoning would be necessary in contravention of the sub-regional plan, and that a possible conflict of interest was involved. Both the school board and regional board disliked the location. Citizens already full of exasperation began to laugh at the extent of the continued bungling.

Still more sites on the west side of the village were taken under consideration, including Rockwood Lodge, but all were rejected. Then Gibsons Council repeated its offer of property to the school board "if they want to come back home." On October 11 the school board opted out of the joint concept and decided to remain in Gibsons. On November 8 they changed their minds and indicated their willingness to talk again about a joint office facility, but on November 26 they voted once more against the project.

In February 1980 a group of doctors made a private proposal for a joint facility on Wharf Road between Cowrie and Dolphin, but the idea went nowhere. In June the Indian Band advised that it was planning a multi-use centre and invited the regional board to consider the complex as a possible alternative for the joint

Village of Sechelt and SCRD office building. The board, however, voted in favour of remaining with the site adjacent to the sewage treatment plant.

Expansion

IN JUNE 1980, plans for the buildings next door to the marsh went back to the designer for redrawing and pricing. Sechelt council was concerned with mounting costs due to delay and decided to have contingency plans drawn for a possible thousand-square-foot addition to the north end of its existing hall.

In September 1980 it was learned that working drawings and estimates for the joint office would not be ready for two months. However, former alderman Dennis Shuttleworth had agreed to draw up plans for the proposed expansion of the village office at no cost to council. A

The expansion of the municipal hall in 1981.

Clearing land in 1914 for Sechelt's first park, known as the "Picnic Grounds." The project was undertaken by a German syndicate, the Canadian- European Investment Corporation, who briefly owned Bert Whitaker's property between Trail and Porpoise Bays. This view includes six Sechelt Indians working with crosscut saw, cable, etc., Whitaker House is on the right, the water tower and the rear of the three-storey post office and general store on the left.

preliminary sketch was available at the September 20 meeting.

On October 1, council passed a resolution that the administration building remain in its present location. It was recommended that the structure be extended northward sixteen feet for the full depth of the hall and that a second floor be added. This increased the floor area to 2,760 square feet. A mansard roof was adopted to add character and it was planned to retain the white stucco finish.

Tenders were called in November for return by December 1, at which time the contract was awarded to K. Solli Contracting in the amount of $46,180 for both renovations and new construction.

On the evening of February 4, 1981 council held its regular meeting for the first time in the new chamber. The building was completely paid for in that year and the overrun of about $1,500 was well spent on things like improved windows and soundproofing. The chamber was made with adequate seating space for guests and delegations. After all the looking around for alternative sites, the municipal hall remained where it was.

BERT HACKETT AND SECHELT PARKLAND

THE ORIGINAL PARK IN SECHELT was located in the two-square-block area bounded by Cowrie and Dolphin Streets and Inlet Avenue and Wharf Road. Dolphin west of Wharf had not yet been opened up, so the northern margin of the park straggled off into the woods, but there was a neat wire fence bordering Wharf and curving around Cowrie.

In the early days this tract was known only as the Sechelt Picnic Grounds, to distinguish it from the Selma Park Picnic Grounds. However, before the land was broken up and sold it was often referred to as Sechelt Park.

In 1924 Bert Whitaker hired Robert Simpson Hackett as accountant to run the office of Sechelt Seaside Resort Company. After Herbert Whitaker died in 1925, Bert Hackett stayed on working for the estate, which was managed by the Canadian Credit Men's Trust Association. The Union Steamship Company purchased the Whitaker properties in April 1926, and Mr. Hackett was employed by them or their associated company, Union Estates Limited, for the next twenty-two years.

George H.R. Aman, who had started working for Whitaker around 1902, was the first resident agent in Sechelt for the Union Company, and when he retired in 1928 he was succeeded by Bert Hackett as local superintendent. This involved overall management of the store, hotel, dance pavilions, bath house (by this time enlarged into the Parthenon Restaurant), boat rentals, cottage rentals, tennis and badminton courts and picnic grounds at both the Selma Park and Sechelt resorts.

In March 1952 the parcel of land comprising our original park was surveyed for Union Estates. Subdivision Plan 8643 was prepared and the new lots were placed on the market. Sale of company properties in Selma Park had been underway as early as 1946.

Ernie Parr Pearson was the prime mover behind a request to the Union Steamship Company that they donate land in Sechelt for a replacement park. In March 1952 both the local and Vancouver newspapers carried stories that the Union Company had presented five acres to Sechelt for use as a park and playground to be known as Hackett Park in honour of the late R.S. Hackett.

The letter from the company stipulated that the gift was subject to the com-

Prominent Sechelt citizens seated on the steps of a cottage on the Boulevard during the late 1930s. Back row, left to right: Edward (Teddy) Hill Sr., George H.R. Aman and Duncan Irvine. Front row: Robert Hackett, Marjorie Hackett, Margaret Hill (partly obscured by Mr. Hackett's dog), Jessica Irvine and Mae Whitaker. The Irvines pre-empted District Lot 3259 on the east side of Porpoise Bay in 1912, so the stream running through their property into Sechelt Inlet near Lamb Islets is named Irvine Creek in their honour. Some maps misspell this feature as "Irving." Duncan and Sica's well-furnished bungalow, floating wharf, fine garden and hospitality were widely reknown. George Aman came to Sechelt about 1902 to work for Bert Whitaker, and from 1926 to 1928 he was postmaster and also resident manager in Sechelt for the Union Steamship Company. Teddy Hill was a forest ranger for the BC government. His wife Margaret later taught school in Sechelt and married for a second time.

Bradley Benson photographed the Porpoise Bay Marsh from the air for the *Coast News* in October 1981.

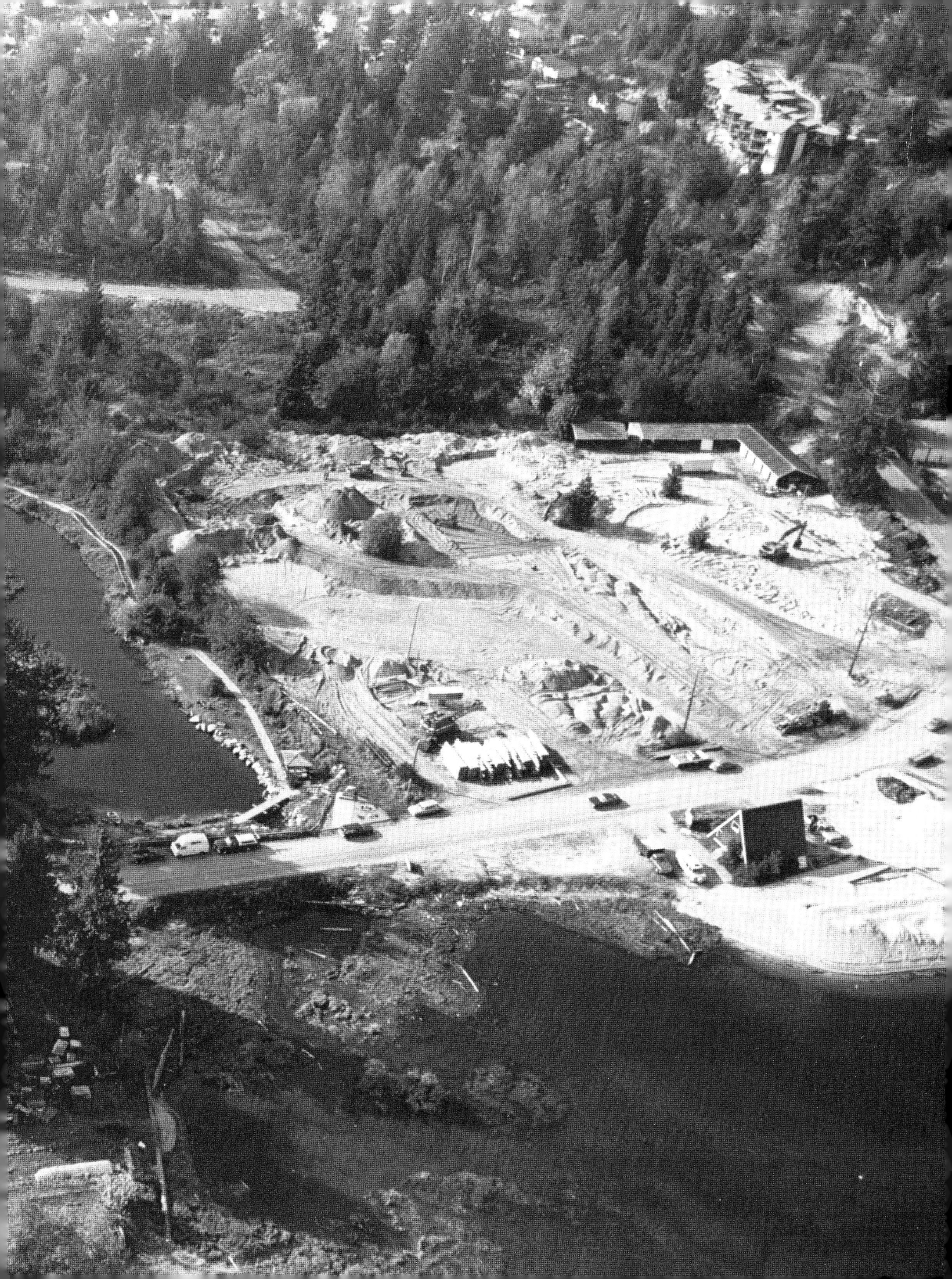

Sechelt's third May Day celebration, held May 24, 1950, Queen Victoria's birthday, on the Union picnic grounds. Our first May Day took place at the Sechelt school on the Porpoise Bay waterfront in 1918, after which there was a hiatus until the custom was revived in 1949. The 1950 May Queen, Mary Parker (Mrs. Cece Gordon), is seen standing in the doorway of the playhouse which was a raffle prize donated to the PTA, sponsors of the ceremonies, by Sechelt Building Supplies (Walker Bros.) and transported aboard a Union Steamship Company truck. With Queen Mary on the porch are her two attendants, Ditty Jay (standing) and Averil Lucken (sitting). The retiring 1949 Queen, Sundi Stroshein, is leaning out a window. The flower girls in front are Barbara Billingsley, Jenny Brown, Donna Dutz, Joyce Gilbertson, Sharon Keeley, Anne Lang, Donna Stubbs and Caroline Watts. Gordon West exhibited his movie truck in the parade and 400 people watched the children dancing around two Maypoles. In 1973 the name of the annual May Day was changed to "Timber Days."

munity putting in proper roads to the park and the clearing of the property for playground purposes. In 1952, Dolphin and Medusa Streets and Ocean and Trail Avenues — the borders of the new park — had not yet been opened up.

Several Sechelt organizations, as well as the Selma Park Community Association, were discussing the building of a community hall for the combined area. Ernie Parr Pearson felt that the new park might provide an ideal site, but the hall never materialized.

The Sechelt Board of Trade was advised by the Union company that the five-acre block would be deeded to the board in trust for the community until such time as Sechelt became an incorporated village, at which time the property would be deeded to the village by the trustee.

The board appointed E.E. Coe as chairman of its parks committee and he organized successful clearing bees. A large ball field was prepared and adjoining roads were built with generous donations of labour and money from the community. Ted Osborne, Sr. supervised the work and he and Jackson Brothers Logging lent equipment.

Letters patent incorporating the Village of Sechelt were granted on February 15, 1956 and in May the board of trade asked the Union company to transfer title to Hackett Park directly to the village. On August 21, 1957 the Union company advised the village commission that survey work had commenced at the park site. The deed did not arrive in Sechelt until December 5, 1957. It contained a "specific covenant not to use the land for any purposes other than a municipal public park without the consent of Union Steamships Ltd." The first report of municipal activities for the period ending December 1956 stated that "Request was made to the Union Steamships Ltd. to permit the acquisition by the Village, through purchase or otherwise, of the half-block of property comprising approximately 2½ acres adjoining Hackett Park to the North–and thus increase the Park area to a size in keeping with the foreseeable needs of the Village." Nothing was accomplished in this matter and houses now cover the area on the north side of Medusa Street.

By July 1958 a start had been made on fencing the park and the Kinsmen Club was preparing children's playground facilities. In 1960 a backstop and flagpole were installed and the park was used for the first time for ballgames and May Day celebrations.

As part of 1958's BC Centennial celebrations the village sponsored a project to do further clearing, erect bleachers and seed the area. During the ensuing decade a stage was erected, power poles installed, tennis courts and a horseshoe pitch constructed and a tire tree completed. On May 21 and 22, 1978, the sixth annual Sechelt Timber Days were celebrated with many events staged in the park.

Other Parkland

IN THE EARLY 1980S the 160-acre Kinnikinnick Park was established. This largely wooded park was named by Billie Steele after a red-berried shrub found locally. Snickett Park, at the westerly end of the Boulevard, is named for an English phrase meaning "little trail." Annie Whitely, an Englishwoman who lived near the park would occasionally look out her window and comment that someone was going "through the snickett."

SECHELT MARSH

IN 1964 the voters of Sechelt defeated a plebiscite on the proposed acquisition of Porpoise Bay shoreline property at $28,000 for a park. Over the years private interests dumped stumps, mill ends, sawdust and other refuse into considerable portions of the marsh. In July 1973 Rivtow Straits, in conjunction with the Seaway Estates company, proposed to turn the swamp area into a lakeshore with private lots fronting it and boats on the lake. Glenmont Holdings issued a plan showing a similar disruptive treatment of the marsh.

Members of the Sechelt Marsh Protection Society work to make paths accessible to wheelchairs in October, 1981.

"Nellie and Joey, Porpoise Bay, Aug. 1898" is the identification appearing on the back of the original print from which this picture was copied. The words were inscribed by Sarah Belle Cook, my grandmother, who died in Sechelt in 1918. The horses were the property of Bert Whitaker, who also owned the land where Nellie and Joey grazed. They fed on the lagoon grasses, which were once a natural portion of the Sechelt Marsh on its western side near the present government wharf. Harry Roberts, of the family for whom Roberts Creek is named, purchased Nellie from Whitaker after the latter acquired a team. Harry had a contract to supply Whitaker with cordwood for the SS *Newera*, which steamed between Vancouver and Sechelt, commencing in 1903. Harry employed his brother to cut the wood and he used Nellie to haul the fuel to a scow.

To offset the indifference of citizens and developers alike, Alderman Norman Watson took the initiative in gathering together a group of people who would work to keep the marsh a sanctuary. He attracted to Sechelt John Rodgers, ornithologist and wildlife columnist, who felt that the slough should be left intact as a nesting ground for birds. Rodgers met with council and explained how the entire ecological chain at the head of Porpoise Bay could be affected by destruction of the marsh. Not only birds but fish would suffer if the rich intertidal feeding area were disturbed.

The village contacted R.D. Harris, biologist with the Canadian Wildlife Service, to inspect the marsh in October 1973. Mr. Harris reported to council that a grant for a marsh program might be secured from the National Second Century Fund of BC. In 1975 the fund made $50,000 available for the purchase of the marsh property and its development. The village acquired a 99-year lease but does not hold title to the land.

The Sechelt Marsh Protective Society was incorporated in September 1976 with Norm Watson as one of the six charter members. The village entrusted the care of the marsh to the society and has given grants in aid of maintenance and improvements.

Jack and Lee Redman's store, with the side entrance to the public library at the top of the stairs.

These three floathouses were intended to be used for the original hospital at Pender Harbour. They were, however, ruined while being towed through Johnstone Straits in 1929.

LIBRARIES

THE FIRST LIBRARY in Sechelt was a private lending library operated by Alice French in a cottage she owned on the north side of Cowrie Street east of Inlet Avenue. The first public library in Sechelt opened on September 21, 1961 and was housed in a second-storey apartment above Jack and Lee Redman's Sechelt Service Store between Inlet and Trail Avenues. The Redmans once lived in the apartment but moved and allowed the library to use it free of charge. The building was later sold to the Chain Saw Centre and the upper storey was demolished. The only access was by way of a steep stairway on the west side of the building.

The second home of the public library opened on April 28, 1966 in a cottage on the south side of Cowrie between Inlet and Trail. This building was eventually sold and moved to Trail Bay. Centennial Library was opened on December 17, 1967, and underwent improvements in 1971.

HOSPITALS

MEMBERS OF THE PENDER HARBOUR community and Reverend John Antle of the Columbia Coast Mission met together in 1929 and agreed to station a hospital there. Three floathouses were to have been brought over from O'Brien Bay and altered into a five-bed hospital, but they were wrecked while being towed in Johnstone Strait in a storm in July 1929.

Nothing daunted, funds were collected and St. Mary's Hospital was constructed at Garden Bay in 1929–30 at a cost of $25,000 on land donated by R. Brynildsen, Sr.

Extended Care Unit →

Deliveries

↑ Staff Parking

↑ Emergency

↑

Pictured here in 1990, twenty-six years after its opening, Sechelt's St. Mary's Hospital continues to serve the entire Sechelt Peninsula.

St. Mary's Hospital, Garden Bay. Originally the only hospital on the Sunshine Coast, it was closed and replaced by St. Mary's hospital at Sechelt in November 1964.

Lieutenant Governor R.R. Bruce formally opened the institution on August 16, 1930, at which time St. Mary's contained twelve beds, two solariums, a maternity room, nursery, caseroom and operating room. The Reverend Mr. Antle provided the initiative and impetus which resulted in cooperation by the Pender Harbour citizens, governments, and the Anglican church to achieve a much-needed medical service. At the same time the federal government built Hospital Wharf at Garden Bay. The provincial government built a short road with a retaining wall leading to the hospital, but it was not until 1941 that 8,400 feet of road was completed linking Garden Bay with the main highway to Irvines Landing. It was often easier for clients to arrive by water than travel the rough roads along the Sechelt Peninsula. On November 30, 1964 the original St. Mary's was closed and the patients transferred to the new hospital at Sechelt, built on land donated by the Indian Band.

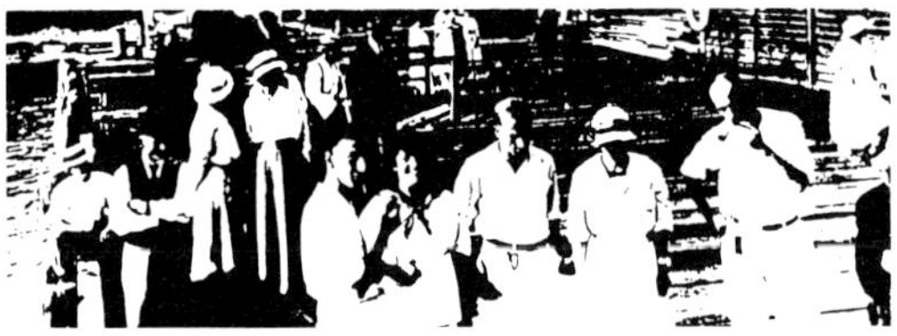

SCHOOLS AND CHURCHES

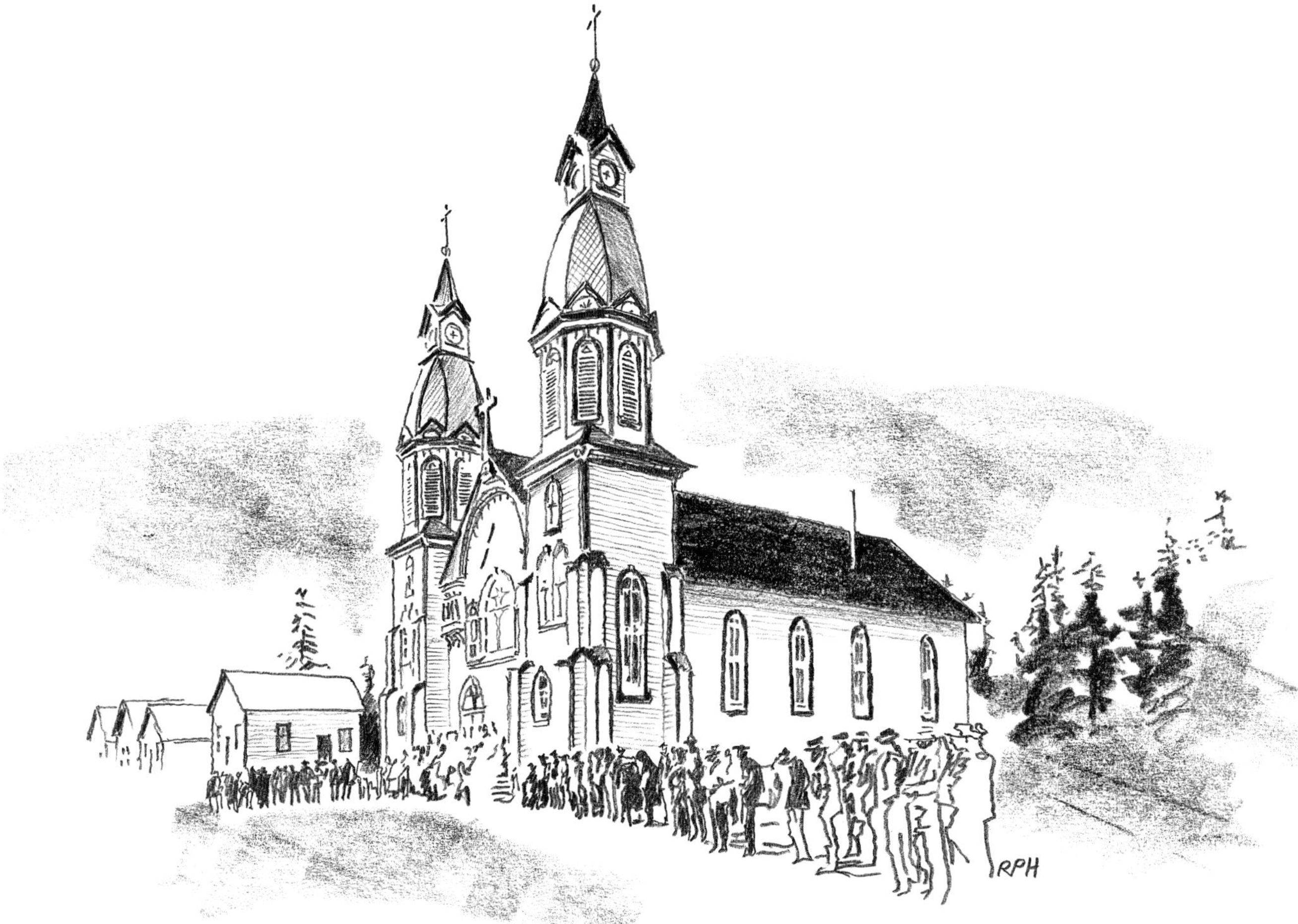
RPH

ST. AUGUSTINE'S:
The First Sechelt Residential School

THE FEDERAL GOVERNMENT estimated the population of the Sechelt tribes around the turn of the century to be between 236 and 325. In the years 1902 to 1904, this small group from various communities on the southern coast planned, financed and erected a large three-storey wooden school. Their own initiative and labour also provisioned the school for a period.

The dedication services at the school's opening were presided over by Father Augustine Dontenwill, the Bishop of New Westminster, on June 29, 1904, and the building was named St. Augustine's in honour of Bishop Dontenwill's patron saint. A number of Sisters of the Child Jesus came out to British Columbia from France in 1903 to instruct at the school in 1904.

The main building could accommo-

St. Augustine's residential school, beautifully situated on top of a small hill overlooking Trail Bay. The three-storey wooden structure cost $11,000 and was paid for by the Indians themselves with funds earned from logging and fishing. It opened in 1904 and was destroyed by fire in 1917.

date sixty pupils plus staff, and measured eighty-three by thirty-six feet with a wing thirty by twenty-eight feet in the rear, which contained a chapel. When the Sisters of the Child Jesus arrived in Sechelt to staff the school at its opening in the summer of 1904, one of their order wrote: "We immediately went to the chapel where there were as yet neither chairs nor pews. As substitute we used a plank upheld at each end by a crate." The finished chapel featured a painted ceiling, gracefully shaped windows, elegant religious statues and handsomely carved pews. The service building behind included playrooms, laundry, workshops and woodsheds, and there was also a stable. An orchard was planted in front of the school and there was a thriving vegetable garden. It was necessary, however, to supplement the game and fish and home-grown fare with purchases from Bert Whitaker's store.

The language of instruction at the

Indian Boarding School, Sechelt, B.C.

Students at the Sechelt Indian residential school St. Augustine's in early 1917 with the priest, father William Brabender, OMI. Mary Jane Pinchbeck (later well-known as Mrs. Mary Jackson, basket maker) stands in the third row from the rear, fourth student from the left. Clarence Joe (born December 1908) is the third boy from the right in the third row from the front. His brother, Stanley Joe, is immediately left of Father Brabender. The girl second from left in the front row is Sarah Paul, later Mrs. Sarah Silvey of Egmont. In 1935 Father Brabender published a history of the Sechelt Mission, written in French.

This chapel occupied the third floor of the rear wing of the wooden St. Augustine's Residential School from 1905 until the building was destroyed by fire in 1917. This photo was copied from the collection of David Paul, who was pupil No. 6 at the school and who died in Sechelt in 1981, aged 87 years.

early Indian school was English; at home the children spoke their own distinctive dialect of the Salishan linguistic group; and the original sisters spoke French. Somehow they managed to work together and achieve a great deal.

Very early in the morning of May 29, 1917 the Sechelt Indian Residential School was completely destroyed by fire. Gladys Tidy, who taught in the public school in Sechelt at the time, described the blaze: "I was living at the hotel at the time and there was a real hubbub for a while. The nuns were wonderful that night helping to evacuate the building, although I don't think there were many children in residence at that time of year. Bert Whitaker took the 'refugees' all in to the hotel till they found other lodging."

Severe privations were suffered for a time after the fire. A nun who was present at the 1917 fire remembered that after the fire the sisters occupied shacks without windows. Mrs. Ada Dawe recalled that some of the nuns lived in square tents with rough board floors elevated above the ground by the width of about three planks. All their possessions were lost and so temporary shoes were made, utilizing as soles several layers of felt cut from old hats donated by friends.

The location of the residential school was moved to two temporary buildings

The third Sechelt Indian residential school, which was erected circa 1920 to 1922 and was demolished in 1975, shown here about 1926.

until a new school was constructed between 1920 and 1922. The new school, also called St. Augustine's, was made of brick, but was ultimately demolished in 1975.

SECHELT'S FIRST PUBLIC SCHOOL

THE ESTABLISHMENT of Sechelt's first public school took place in 1912, on the initiative of Mr. T.J. Cook. The provincial government advised that it would pay a teacher's salary if the villagers would make a building available and supply desks.

Two young ladies, Mattie Nickson and Ada Cook, held a tag day and collected sufficient funds to purchase the desks. The loggers were generous and Bert Whitaker permitted the school to use a small two-storey building on the Boulevard, just west of Wharf Avenue. He had built it originally as his second store at the time he opened his nearby hotel in 1899. The structure had been used as a bunkhouse after Mr. Whitaker erected a much larger store in 1905–06 on the site of the present oil tank farm.

The first teacher was Grace Kent, who came to Sechelt from Vancouver in 1912 at the age of nineteen. One of her friends recalled: "She lived in the hotel, and paid twenty dollars per month for room and board. There were dancing parties every Saturday night and many of the young surveyors from the area who stayed at the hotel attended. There were surveyors in the room next to hers at one time and they would tie tin cans together on a long string, dangle them out the window and frighten everyone with the noise they

The building to the left on the Boulevard west of Wharf Avenue was Sechelt's first school in 1912 and first telegraph office in 1913. It was erected by Bert Whitaker in 1899 as a store and post office. This photo is from the period between 1914 and 1918, during which time Bert Whitaker constructed the building bearing the general store sign. The two shops were then joined together, with the older store housing the butcher's department. The Whitaker horses have just pulled a wagon off the wharf. Our Lady of Lourdes Indian church (1907–1970) appears in the background. Photo by Charles Bradbury, Sechelt's telegrapher.

made banging on the building. Until she found out what it was Grace always pushed the dressing table in front of her door. Her pupils played tricks on her as well. Once the boys fastened a dead rat inside the armhole of her heavy coat. When she put it on she couldn't figure out what was wrong until she got outside—then she dropped it off and ran all the way home."

The Sechelt school probably commenced about mid-October 1912 and was in session for only 162½ days during the academic year. Miss Kent received a salary of sixty dollars per month. The local district expended nothing in addition. Sechelt's first seat of learning was classified as an "Assisted School" and it was within Inspectorate No. 5, which extended from Prince Rupert and the Charlottes down the rural portions of the coast. Understandably the inspector had time to pay only one visit to the Sechelt

PORPOISE BAY, SECHELT, B. C.

School. Miss Kent's class consisted of 11 boys and 7 girls, a total of 18 pupils, but the average daily attendance was only 12.5.

The pupils came from the settlements at Selma Park, Porpoise Bay, and Norw-

Back to school at Sechelt in 1913 meant classes in this rough building on the Porpoise Bay waterfront where the tide came up under the floor. Fortunately by December 1914 volunteer labour had erected a new schoolhouse at the other end of the footbridge across the stream flowing out of the Sechelt marsh.

PORPOISE BAY SECHELT B C

The northern portion of the dusty Porpoise Bay Road is seen here in 1915, long before its name was changed to Wharf Avenue. Where it dips out of sight it turned left across the open mouth of the lagoon now known as the Sechelt Marsh. At high tide a horse hauling freight or passengers from this point toward the original Porpoise Bay wharf would have to wade through water up to the deck of the wagon. The wharf is hidden by trees bordering the lagoon. The building at the head of the bay was the second home of the Sechelt school, built originally as the Yamamoto Boat Works, while the building on the right is the newly constructed third school.

est (now Sargeant) Bay. They walked considerable distances along trails or skid roads from West Sechelt or from isolated farms or logging camps along the shores of the inlet. Others rowed across Porpoise Bay. Those who travelled farthest were Lawrence Molberg and two Morse boys, who walked daily from Sargeant Bay to the Sechelt school, travelling along the beach and crossing Wakefield Creek on a log. They reached T.J. Cook's home near the beach promptly at 8:35 a.m. and stopped to check with his clock. The boys were never absent or tardy. Lawrence was the son of Lewis Molberg, a deckhand on the *Tartar*, so when the steamer

Gladys Tidy, who taught school in Sechelt in 1917 and 1918, is pictured here at the Trail Bay waterfront in 1917, at the age of 17.

had occasion to travel upcoast from Sechelt during the afternoon, Miss Kent would release the three boys a little early from class so that they might enjoy a ride home.

The first schoolhouse was used only from the autumn of 1912 to Easter 1913. In May of 1913 the telegraph office took

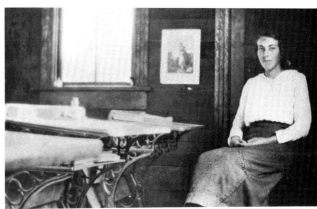

Islay Findlay sitting inside the third Sechelt public school in 1918, on Wharf Road near Osprey Street.

over the building because the federal government was willing to pay Bert Whitaker seven dollars per month rent for the space.

Miss Kent and her pupils then moved to a shack at the head of Porpoise Bay just west of the present wildlife sanctuary at the marsh. The tide came up under the floor of this building, which had been used by Japanese fishermen to repair their boats and nets. When Dr. Fred Inglis of Gibsons made his medical inspection for the year ending June 1914 he reported that the building was poor and draughty, the heating bad, and that there were no sanitary closets. The health of the pupils was also less than desirable. Of the nine girls and boys examined, one suffered from malnutrition, seven had defective teeth, three had adenoids, three enlarged tonsils and three enlarged glands.

A new building was made available near the end of 1914, located on Wharf Avenue at the Porpoise Bay waterfront. The school there had three teachers in the year 1916–17. They were paid sixty-five dollars a month to instruct a class of 131

nineteen. Another teacher, Gladys Tidy, arrived in Sechelt in January 1917 at the age of nineteen and left the area at the end of 1918. This school served the area until 1920, when a school was built on the Norwest Bay hill in the vicinity of Nickerson Road, an area where many families were settling after the First World War. The school was constructed for the cost of $350 on land donated by Bill Mitchell, a World War I veteran. Frank French, the son of W.J. French, one of Sechelt's earliest school trustees, and a group of other men living in the neighbourhood joined together to do the actual building of the school. The original structure was probably about 30 by 25 feet.

The first teacher in the new school was Florence Cliff, who had arrived in Sechelt in 1919 and earned a monthly salary of eighty dollars. Robert C. Kean and his brother Alex expanded this school sometime in the later 1920s. In the late 1930s Alex Kean, who drove a truck for the Union Steamship Company, was enlisted by the local school board to provide transportation to and from the West Sechelt school. He picked the youngsters

Sechelt school circa 1930. The old school was located just east of Nickerson Road on Norwest Bay Road (formerly School Road) in West Sechelt, and is often confused with West Sechelt School, which wasn't built until 1960. It was later moved to the present Sechelt schoolground in 1946, where it still serves as a kindergarten.

up at Cowrie Street and Inlet Avenue in the old open Union truck and drove them along the rough gravelled road. The truck lacked not only sides but formal seats as well. It was, however, a vast improvement on the long climb up the Norwest Bay hill on foot in all weathers and home again through the dark woods on a winter's afternoon.

The original West Sechelt schoolhouse was used for almost twenty years and was superseded by Sechelt United School, where both elementary and secondary school students were taught. Opening ceremonies in this new institution, located between Cowrie and Dolphin Streets and Ocean and Shorncliffe Avenues, were held on March 6, 1939. Efforts to sell the old schoolhouse on Norwest Bay road were without success and the building was boarded up for seven years. In 1946 the old building was moved down to face Shorncliffe Avenue, where it was used as a kindergarten. In 1976 the building was moved once again to face Cowrie Street, and was initially painted in a colour which one student described aptly but inelegantly as "shitty brown," not an aesthetically pleasing hue. Nonetheless, this is one pioneer building which the citizens of Sechelt have loved sufficiently well to preserve.

Opening ceremonies at Sechelt United school, opened at Cowrie Street and Shorncliffe Avenue on March 6, 1939.

A dinner in the dining room of the first Sechelt Hotel circa 1912. Those present include H.M. Bennett, an employee of Bert Whitaker's, standing in front of the window on the right, and Edie Morgan (later Mrs. Stanley Delong), the girl turned to face the camera. Note the hanging gas lamps.

A Sechelt Christmas in 1912

IN THE WINTERS of the years preceding World War I the residents of Sechelt, Selma Park and Porpoise Bay included a core of about a dozen permanent families plus a variety of transient loggers, prospectors, surveyors, hunters, a teacher, a game warden and the employees in Bert Whitaker's store, hotel, mill and other various enterprises. The Sechelt Indian Band numbered about 240 persons, mainly occupied in fishing and logging up the inlets. Their school and church on Reserve No. 2 were served by a handful of nuns from France and a resident Oblate priest.

At Christmas most of the casuals left to celebrate in Vancouver. The neighbours who remained visited among themselves and made their own entertainment. The arrival of parcels and letters from distant families and friends made the thrice-weekly arrival of the mail in Sechelt particularly exciting. Special orders of holly and pheasant-eyed narcissi, a favoured Christmas flower early in the century, were brought in, as were Japanese oranges, a seasonal treat in 1912 as they are now, though then they cost only 35 cents per box. And everyone noticed the Christmas trees attached to the masts of each of the many tugs passing by or sheltering their booms in Trail Bay.

The Sechelt Indians issued invitations to their white neighbours to attend a Christmas concert at the original residential school. There was a tree, the Indian brass band played and all the students participated in singing carols, reciting poems and performing the little tableaux so popular at the time. Refreshments were served, after which the guests proceeded home on foot, their way lit by coal-oil lanterns. Every Christmas Chief Julius, hereditary chief of the Sqaiaqos clan of the Sechelt Nation, paid a visit to Thomas John Cook, and the two friends drank a toast together, though it was illegal at the time to offer a glass of spirits to a native person.

Bert Whitaker, as was his annual custom, extended invitations to a Christmas dinner held in the dining room of his Sechelt Hotel overlooking Trail Bay. The dining room in the hotel was finished with an elaborately designed wallpaper and the windows were draped with lace curtains. One dining table at Christmas 1912 was decorated with four vases of narcissi. The paintings on the walls were displayed in gilt frames. One picture is said to have been painted by a member of the Group of Seven who gave the work to Bert Whitaker in payment of his hotel bill. This story may be apocryphal but the Whitaker family did indeed have a fine collection of paintings of local scenery, executed by the established BC artists of the day.

CHURCHES:
The Five Churches of the Sechelt Band

WHEN THE SECHELT INDIAN PEOPLE were converted to Christianity during the early 1860s they built many small chapels along Jervis and Sechelt inlets and at Pender Harbour. Their first place of worship on what is now the Sechelt Indian Band Lands, was a wooden Roman Catholic chapel built in 1868 on the Trail Bay waterfront. Since that time, with the exception of brief intervals, there has always been a house of worship on the same site. The two buildings between 1868 and 1889 may more properly be referred to as chapels, but the three edifices thereafter have the dignity of important churches.

The Sechelt Nation had been con-

Bishop Paul Durieu, OMI.

An outdoor Roman Catholic altar on the Trail Bay shoreline of Sechelt Indian Reserve No. 2 early in the century. Such altars were set up over a long period of years for masses celebrating Corpus Christi. Even though the Indian people had built themselves a series of churches near Trail Bay dating back to 1869, Mrs. Carrie Joe (née Johnson) and Mrs. Mary Martha Joe (née August) recalled that as late as the 1930s five outdoor altars were set up for Corpus Christie rites, one for each of the five hereditary chiefs of the Sechelt Nation. This was after the five septs or divisions of the people had been amalgamated in 1926. Note the formal dark suits worn by the kneeling men and the shawls wrapped around the shoulders of the Indian ladies. The point of land just right of centre is Holy Joe's Rock, to which the "Selma" was anchored in 1916. During the 1960s the rock became a harbour of refuge built by the federal government. Its construction obscured the graceful natural curve of the beach in front of the reserve.

A view of Sechelt from what was then called Government Road, now Highway 101, likely around 1913–1914.

42 - VIEW FROM THE GOVERNMENT ROAD
SECHELT, B.C.

verted to Roman Catholicism by Father (later Bishop) Paul Durieu, OMI. He had arrived at Olympia in 1854 at the age of twenty-five on assignment to the Oregon mission of the Oblates. With the establishment of the Crown Colony of British Columbia in 1858, Father Louis D'Herbomez, who had served in the neighbouring American area, became superior over the new missions in BC as well, and led his priests in their work among the native people. Father Durieu and another priest, Father Fouquet, arrived at Vancouver Island on December 12, 1859. The early evangelists to the Sechelt Nation also included Father Eugene Casimir Chirouse, who had reached Oregon in 1847.

Father Jean-Marie LeJeune came to BC in 1879 and trained for two years under Bishop Durieu, working among the Sechelt and the Stalo Indians, who lived in the Fraser Valley area. He became adept in the use of the Chinook jargon, a trade language, which in spite of its very limited vocabulary was used to communicate the Gospels. The Indians spoke their own dialects; the mother tongue of the early priests was French; while the so-called white settlers used not only English spoken in a variety of accents, but many other languages as well. The interchange of thoughts cannot have been easy.

Because the small number of pioneer priests found it difficult to visit all the separate scattered communities by boat, it was suggested that the Sechelt people select a central place where they could join together for the celebration of special Christian occasions. So it was that the four ancient divisions or "septs" of the Nation (Hunechin, from the head of Queen's Reach, Jervis Inlet; Tsonai, who lived at Deserted Bay and Jervis Inlet; Tuwanek, from Narrows Arm and adjacent areas; and Sqaiaqos, who had many settlements but no fixed abode) all gathered at Chatelech to build a chapel and two dwelling places in 1868. A new vil-

Sechelt Indians performing one of the tableaux constituting the Passion Play, around 1890. Their open-air platform stood on the grounds of Saint Mary's Mission with the Fraser River in the background. The man on the far left playing a Roman Soldier was "Policeman Paul," grandfather of Sarah Silvey of Egmont. The lady in white clasping the foot of the cross was Tutla, known also as Molly, wife of the great Chief Julius and grandmother of Carrie Joe. Note second actor from left holding mallet and nails used to secure Christ upon the cross.

lage grew up on the site of the former community, which had almost been exterminated by smallpox. With the passage of time the name Chatelech fell into disuse and the village became known as Sechelt, in honour of the Indian Nation which gathered around the mission founded there by Bishop Durieu.

The second Indian Roman Catholic chapel at Sechelt is reported to have been underway by August 1872 because the original 1868 building had already become too small for the congregation. The new structure measured 49 feet long by 23 feet wide. This chapel was named SS. Redempteur, or Church of the Holy Redeemer. It was subsidiary to the Mission of St. Charles on the Fraser at New Westminster. The second Sechelt church was blessed by Father Durieu on April 15, 1873.

In addition to Our Lady of the Rosary, the Sechelts erected a two-storey house for the missionaries, located just back and to the west of the new church. The SS. Redempteur church still stood just behind the priests' house, but by 1893 it had been converted into a catechism house. Although I am not certain of the date, it was probably some time before the turn of the century that SS. Redempteur was converted into a meeting hall. Here such notable leaders as Chief Julius, Chief Tom and Chief George consulted together, dispensed justice and transacted business with government representatives. Here too, the Band as a whole gathered to participate in decision-making. In the mid-1930s fire destroyed both the priests' house—which at the time was occupied by Clarence Joe, son of Basil Joe—and the SS. Redempteur.

The third Sechelt Indian church, the most imposing of all the five edifices on the site, was described by Father A.G. Morice in his *History of the Catholic Church in Western Canada* as follows:

The Sechelt Indian Band brass band on the steps of an unidentified building, perhaps in New Westminster or Vancouver. Note the fascinating carved wooden chain ornaments decorating the entrance. The date is probably the late 1890s. Band leader Frank Isidore appears on the right end of the third row from the front, wearing civilian garb. In 1904 Charles Hill-Tout published a report on the ethnology of the Sechelts, including five generations of the family tree of Chief Julius Lamquatci III, pictured in the centre of the front row. Julius was hereditary chief of the Sqaiaqos clan, which had many settlements. He was educated at St. Mary's Mission before the Sechelts built their own school, and later spent much of his time at Wilson Creek, where he protected the native fishery and was prominent in consultations with the government. Mrs. Carrie Joe, granddaughter of Chief Julius, made this photo available.

"The crowning glory of the model village was a church 80 feet by 28, with a facade 48 feet wide and two beautiful towers. Commenced October 26, 1889, the building was ready for dedication by June 3, 1890."

Five chiefs, on behalf of their respective coastal communities, made a joint effort to plan the twin-spired church. They were Chief Tom, Chief Johnnie, Chief Alexis, Chief Captain Charlie and Chief Julius, who consulted together at Sechelt and then journeyed to New Westminster to confer with the priests there. Today one can pay one's respects at the gravesides of the chiefs in the Sechelt Indian Cemetery.

Father Morice reported that more than a dozen tribes sent deputations to assist at the dedication of the new Sechelt church by Bishop Durieu. There was a fireworks display, cannons were fired and several brass bands assembled. Players in the Sechelt band wore gorgeous uniforms and they had "a commodious stand for the discoursing of sweet music on Sundays and holidays." In 1890 Frank Isidore was bandmaster of the Sechelt group, which provided music not only for the blessing of the new church, called Our Lady of the Rosary, at home but also for Roman Catholic occasions in other areas.

On June 5, 1890 the *Daily News-Advertiser*, a Vancouver paper, ran a story entitled "The Sechelt Festival." This report doubled the cost of building the church (Father Morice claimed it cost three thousand dollars) and read in part as follows:

Yesterday morning the dedicatory services in connection with the new Roman Catholic Mission Church on Sechelt Island [sic] took place. Shortly before 10 o'clock the procession through the village, in which over two thousand natives marched, took place. The church is

Construction of Our Lady of the Rosary Church commenced in October 1889. It was the third Roman Catholic church built by the Sechelt Indians on the Trail Bay waterfront. The edifice was blessed in June of 1890 and destroyed by fire in January 1906. The Sechelts had founded their brass band in 1888 and later provided it with a bandstand in front of the church.

The interior of Our Lady of the Rosary church in 1904.

People leaving Our Lady of the Rosary church in the summer of 1904 after the dedication of St. Augustine's residential school.

this occasion, of course, it cannot be used for the regular religious services as not a quarter of the number at present in the village can find accommodation. For this reason a large tent in which a temporary altar is placed, has been erected along side. The architect of the new Church is Mr. A. Boulton [sic; a Mr. Bouillon, an architect who had previously worked with members of the Sechelt Band in New Westminster and who lived in the area of Wakefield Creek, was likely the name of the architect who worked on the church] and the Indians themselves did the work of construction under his supervision.

For the present celebration arrangements have been going on for many weeks, and from the interior and all parts of the coast and Vancouver Island the natives have been gathering to take part in this religious festival. Preparations on an elaborate scale have been made for the proper celebration of the event. A large number of native Bands have gathered and fire works have

a very handsome structure, costing over $6,000, and the natives are very proud of it. The interior furnishings are very elaborate and handsome. On the walls are pictures of great events in church history, and the altar and chancel are tastefully ornamented. The whole room evinces the work and attention of pious hands, skillful in ornamentation. The building is capable of holding 450 without crowding. For

been provided in abundance. For the convenience of those coming from the Interior arrangements were made with the CPR for reduced rates and for the week of the festival the *Yosemite* has been chartered by the Bishop to run from Vancouver."

The *Daily World* reported that six brass bands were in attendance and that the Sechelt Indians greeted their guests arriving on the *Yosemite* by striking up a lively air. A display of fireworks was presented in the evening. After dark the Squamish Indians arrived off Mission Point in fifty canoes tied in line, illuminated by Chinese lanterns, and towed by the tug *Leanora*. This procession doubled back across the harbour, carrying its own band in the centre canoe, while the Squamish in other canoes sent off rockets and contributed songs. Miniature cannons were fired from various points along the shoreline.

The 1890 gathering at Sechelt was sadly interrupted by the death of Bishop D'Herbomez on June 3. Bishop Durieu, all the Indian chiefs and dignitaries, many of the Oblates and three Indian brass bands journeyed to New Westminster to participate in the funeral service. After the burial the religious celebrations at Sechelt were resumed.

On January 14, 1906 disaster struck and the sixteen-year-old church burned to the ground. Although the Sechelt Band had brought water down from the hills in an open flume to pipes laid on the reserve as early as the 1890s, the facility was not adequate to fight fire in the tall church towers. A fund to rebuild was sponsored at once.

The fourth church, the single-spired Our Lady of Lourdes, instilled a feeling of profound reverence and affection in countless people from 1907 to 1970. The tall white tower was pointed out to people aboard vessels sailing up the coast and

Sechelt Indian Cemetery, blessed by Reverend Father Paul Durieu, OMI, on April 15, 1873. SS. Redempteur church, dedicated at the same time, can be seen behind Our Lady of Lourdes Church. It is the small domed building observable just to the left of the cross. Eventually it became the band meeting hall.

The last of the hereditary chiefs of the Sechelt people on the steps of Our Lady of the Rosary church in the early 1900s. Front row, left to right: Chief Tom of Deserted Bay; Violet Williams (later Violet Jackson); her father, Alec Williams; Billy Johnson and Little Joe Wawa. Second row, left to right: Chief George; Jim Alec; Joseph August; Casper John, Chief of the Hunechin at the head of Jervis Inlet; Joseph Dally or La Dally; Charlie Roberts; Chief Justice Johnny Wilson; and Paul Alec, partly hidden. Sitting on the very highest step is Frank Isidore, aka Frank Eugene.

could be observed from Nanaimo. It was photographed by innumerable tourists and postcard-makers from vantage points in airplanes, on wharves, by land and sea. Amateur and professional artists painted pictures of it, journalists galore produced magazine and newspaper articles about it and the old edifice appeared regularly on television. Many babies were baptized, children confirmed, young people married, confessions heard and masses said in the church. The Christmas midnight mass in particular was a great family occasion at Sechelt. Novice nuns took their final vows during beautiful services at Our Lady of Lourdes, and elderly people facing death were comforted to know that old friends would gather in the church to sing the familiar hymns for them. I can remember from the days of my childhood that when the bell in the church tower tolled at an unaccustomed hour the whole small community of Sechelt used to pause while people asked each other who had died.

Planning for Our Lady of Lourdes was initiated shortly after the January 1906 fire. The Indian people of Sechelt did some commercial fishing but were employed primarily in the logging industry. Clarence Joe, who remembered the early white settlers nicknaming the Sechelt Band the "Beaver Tribe" because they were such adept loggers, recalled that "the braves went out to their hand logging camps in order to raise money to build the church. Younger members of the tribe were ordered by the chiefs to help the carpenter boss." From monies earned in the woods they put $9,000 into a building fund, but when they attempted to let a contract the lowest bid received was $22,000. So the men did the work themselves with the assistance of Ellis Hermanson, a boatbuilder and master carpenter, and his brother Ivar, also a carpenter. The Indians, long-time expert woodworkers, had no trouble adapting to European styles of construction. Building materials were brought in by barge and landed on the beach. In 1950 Rev. O.T. Royer initiated the building of a shrine behind the west side of the church. There the statue of the Madonna of Lourdes looked out from a rock niche over a rosary appropriately strung from wooden fishnet floats. This grotto was for many years the scene of annual gatherings of Indians who came for many miles to participate in outdoor services. At present the altar, the figure from the niche, and the pews have been removed, but the grotto was still standing in the early 1970s.

The Sechelt waterfront in 1913. All buildings left of the Indian reserve were owned by Bert Whitaker.

Fire destroyed Our Lady of Lourdes on the night of October 24–25, 1970. It broke out in the church's altar section and spread rapidly. By the time the Sechelt Volunteer Fire Department arrived, flames were spewing through the roof. Fifteen men and three pieces of equipment were used but the frame structure could not be saved. The 126-foot bell tower seemed to last an incredibly long time because it was constructed of timbers reinforced with iron brackets and heavy bolts. The bell itself was distorted by heat and shattered when it fell and hit the ground. The fire had erupted into flames at approximately 12:45 a.m. on a Sunday morning and the tower crumbled just after 3 a.m. At 4 o'clock on Sunday afternoon the ruins were still smouldering.

Almost everything was consumed by the blaze, but one armless and faceless figure of the Madonna survived and was placed outside the home of the George August family on the seafront. Only the faintest tinge of the once vivid blue remained to colour her now dingy robe.

A church restoration fund was immediately proposed and as a result the fifth Indian church at Sechelt was established. Clarence Joe was appointed chairman of a committee consigned to search out possible solutions to the problem of providing accommodation for worship. Many people devoted time and effort toward raising the necessary money, with local priests Father Simpson and Father Fitzgerald participating. The Homemakers Club and the Totem Club were particularly active. The ladies sold baked goods and needlework and organized a church fund raffle, while the men made donations from the proceeds of bingo nights. The Band fund, however, contributed the main portion of the financing.

The cost of erecting a new church on the site was estimated at $100,000, but the Sechelt Band also required funds for housing. A satisfactory solution was arrived at when the Band purchased a Protestant chapel from the RCAF base at Ladner. It measured eighty feet by almost sixty feet at its widest point and could accommodate a congregation of two hundred.

The initial cost, complete with pews, was just under $10,000, but much additional expense was incurred to cover such things as moving, insurance and renovation. On February 6, 1973 the tug *Hustler II* towed the steel barge *Seaspan 821* to a gravel fill landing prepared on the southwest corner of the reserve. The barge's cargo consisted of the church—which had been cut into two sections so it would fit—a facilities wing and three houses, all on wheels.

The chapel was moved to the site of the four earlier Roman Catholic churches on the main reserve of the Sechelt Nation. A

The second Our Lady of Lourdes church after being transported to the Indian village from Ladner in 1973.

concrete foundation was installed and the lower space enclosed. The facilities wing with a room for the care of infants was rejoined to the eastern side of the main structure.

Services in the fifth church commenced in the summer of 1973 and the first wedding occurred on June 23, when Miss Lucy Joe married Mr. Tony Paul. The congregation is made up of both Indian and non-Indian adults and children. Superficially, the appearance of the worshipers has altered greatly since the first church in 1868, but just as the people touched the hand of Father Fouquet in 1868, so now does the priest pass down the central aisle of the church to touch the hands of the parishioners.

The Sechelt Image sitting on the "Fill" after its discovery in 1921.

The Sechelt Image

"THE SECHELT IMAGE" is the name given to a prehistoric relic recognized by anthropologists as one of the most valuable stone carvings in existence. It was discovered in 1921 in the roots under the trunk of an old tree at the "Fill" in Selma Park, aross the highway from the site of the wharf which then existed, and close to the old Union Steamship Company dance pavilion. Boys of the Columbus Club made the find, so the stone was taken to the Knights of Columbus Hall in Vancouver. The image now makes its permanent home in the Centennial Museum near Kitsilano Beach in Vancouver.

The figure, created from igneous rock,

is egg-shaped, measures twelve by twenty inches and weighs about sixty pounds. It has sometimes been described as representing a human mother whose arms enfold her child, but the renowned Professor Charles Hill-Tout was more inclined to believe that the squatting figure portrayed a god or good spirit who protected children.

Anthropologist Wilson Duff believed that the sculpture, which has strong phallic symbolism, may be a sample of "heavy oval boulders (which) were hoisted as feats of male strength by some of the Salish, sometimes at betrothal ceremonies," but that ambiguously "male strength is also mother and child."

Yet another account has it that an Indian boy was playing on the beach at Wakefield, where he was captured by a raiding party from upcoast. When his mother learned of the child's death she drowned herself. The grief-stricken husband had a likeness of his wife and son carved as a memorial.

Mrs. W. Garland Foster wrote of the Sechelt Image in *Museum and Art Notes* in October 1926. She stated that the sculpture, when uncovered, "was immediately claimed by Dan Paull (Hwa-Sal-To) of Sechelt, who recognized it as a mortuary stone of his family, which as an uncle related to him, had disappeared many years ago, during an epidemic of smallpox."

ST. HILDA'S ANGLICAN CHURCH

ON NOVEMBER 15, 1936, St. Hilda's Anglican Church was dedicated by Archbishop Adam Urias DePencier. The church was erected on property donated by Thomas John Cook, and is located on land that also served as Sechelt's first cemetery. Mr. Cook started the burial ground in January 1923 when four-month-old Regnheld Evelyn Davidson died at Doriston and her parents had no alternative site available.

Mr. and Mrs. Davidson wrapped their child's body in a blanket and brought her to Sechelt by boat, because there were few roads in 1923. The family lacked financial resources to continue on to Vancouver, so Mr. Cook gave permission for little Regnheld to be buried on his land, and he himself built her wooden coffin, dug the grave, read the burial service and built a little fence to mark the child's place in the rough terrain. When I was a child we used to place wild flowers there, but over time the grave, situated to the north of St. Hilda's Church, came to be quite unmarked.

The second child to be buried in the cemetery also died during the 1920s, due to a sad accident on her parent's farm. I can only just remember the little girl as being very young, a toddler. Her forename sounded like Ike or Oike, but I am ignorant of both the correct spelling and the exact date of her death. Her parents were Jiro Konishi, known locally as Jim, and Mrs. Hanna Konishi. They brought a Buddhist priest up from Vancouver to conduct the funeral service. Mr. Konishi and Mr. Cook were great personal friends, so again the interment was on Mr. Cook's land.

Mr. Konishi died in Sechelt in October 1939 and was buried beside his little daughter and his old friend Mr. Kawamoto, a fisherman who lived with the Konishi family. It is significant that

The interior of St. Hilda's church in the 1940s or 1950s.

146

Saint Hilda's Anglican Church, Sechelt, on the day it was dedicated, November 15, 1936, by Archbishop Adam Urias DePencier. His summer home in West Sechelt was later converted into the Gamma Phi Beta Camp. Standing in front of the church on Shorncliffe Avenue is Jean Cook (later Mrs. Henry Whitaker), the daughter of Thomas John Cook.

Jiro Konishi, a naturalized Canadian, died only a month after the outbreak of the Second World War, because this meant that he did not have to undergo the trauma suffered by his widow and children when the government removed them from Sechelt and sent them to the interior of the province. Their land was sold to white people who permitted the beloved farm to go to ruin.

When Mrs. Konishi died her ashes were returned to Sechelt for interment in the family plot, and the remains of her son, Seiji, were also buried here after he was drowned in central BC. These five Japanese pioneers of Sechelt are grouped together inside a tidy little stone wall and iron fence, with two ornamental Japanese cherry trees marking the spot.

In the summer of 1930 Mr. Cook conveyed the title of the land on which the Sechelt cemetery sat to the Synod of the Anglican Church of Canada. This gift was made when Mr. Cook was in his sixty-seventh year, because he anticipated that the Anglicans would provide adequate care for the cemetery where the two children had already been buried. St. Hilda's Church was erected some years later and consecrated in November 1936.

Many interesting old timers are buried here, including John Lawrence Gilbert Smith, a professional painter who signed his pictures plain Gilbert Smith, R.S. Hackett, the gentleman for whom Hackett Park is named, as well as Duncan and Jessie Irvine.

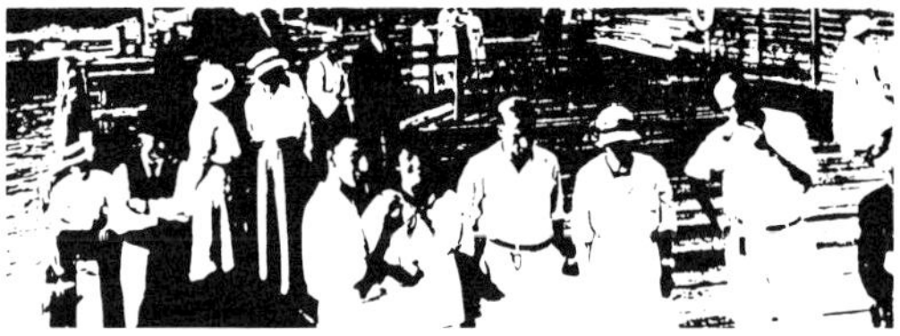

CONCLUSION

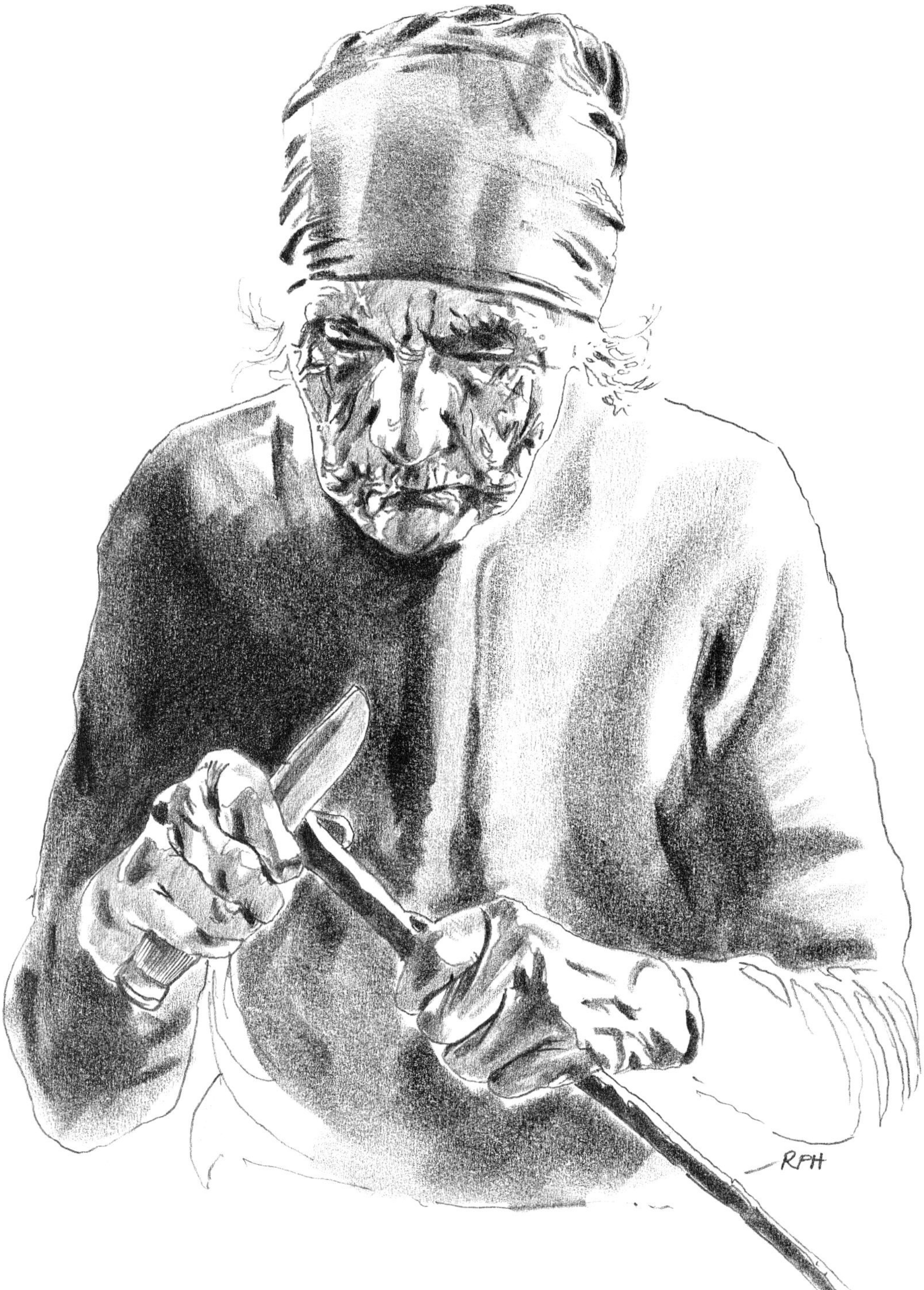
RFH

IN THE CENTURY since settlers like Thomas John Cook and Bert Whitaker first arrived at Sechelt the community has taken root. A steady flow of new residents have expanded Sechelt's borders and population over the years, and have combined with the descendents of some of the original settlers. Together they have established a community that has proven itself resilient enough to survive without those single interests, such as the Whitaker holdings or the Union Steamship Company, that played such a large part in establishing it in the first place. The fact that Sechelt is the seat of political institutions like the SCRD, the site of social institutions such as St. Mary's Hospital, and the site of major commercial projects such as the natural gas pipeline to Vancouver Island seems to indicate that the community's location makes it a natural hub of activity on the Sunshine Coast. But while the village is strong enough to look forward to the future, it must also take care to preserve the memories of the past which shaped it.

Though Sechelt is a small community, its history is not irrelevant, for it reflects the development of the province. The community's settlement by sea mirrors the settlement of numerous communities along the northwest coast. And whether reflected by the early loggers above Selma Park or the tourists at the Union resorts, the economic development of Sechelt is a microcosm of how British Columbia has developed economically. The mixing of peoples of different race and backgrounds—Japanese such as the Konishis; the Swedish Carlsons; the French missionaries and Pete Le Vesque; the American Abe Mason; the Scottish Youngsons and Thomas John Cook of England—is reflective of the cultural makeup of the province and the country. And it can be noted that while people like Bert Whitaker and T.J. Cook demonstrated much foresight in choosing to settle the busy isthmus between Trail Bay and Porpoise Bay, it was the Indian people of Sechelt—currently the only self-governing Indian band in British Columbia—who were the true pioneers in that regard, their tenure in the area being measured not in hundreds but in thousands of years.

So there are things to be learned from how this community developed. But insight can only be gained if an accurate record is kept, based not on myth or rumour but on fact. Hopefully, as Sechelt continues to develop, there will be those willing, to take the time to chronicle its development, and those ready to appreciate that by preserving important connections to its past the community is nourishing its own roots.

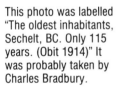

This photo was labelled "The oldest inhabitants, Sechelt, BC. Only 115 years. (Obit 1914)" It was probably taken by Charles Bradbury.

Index

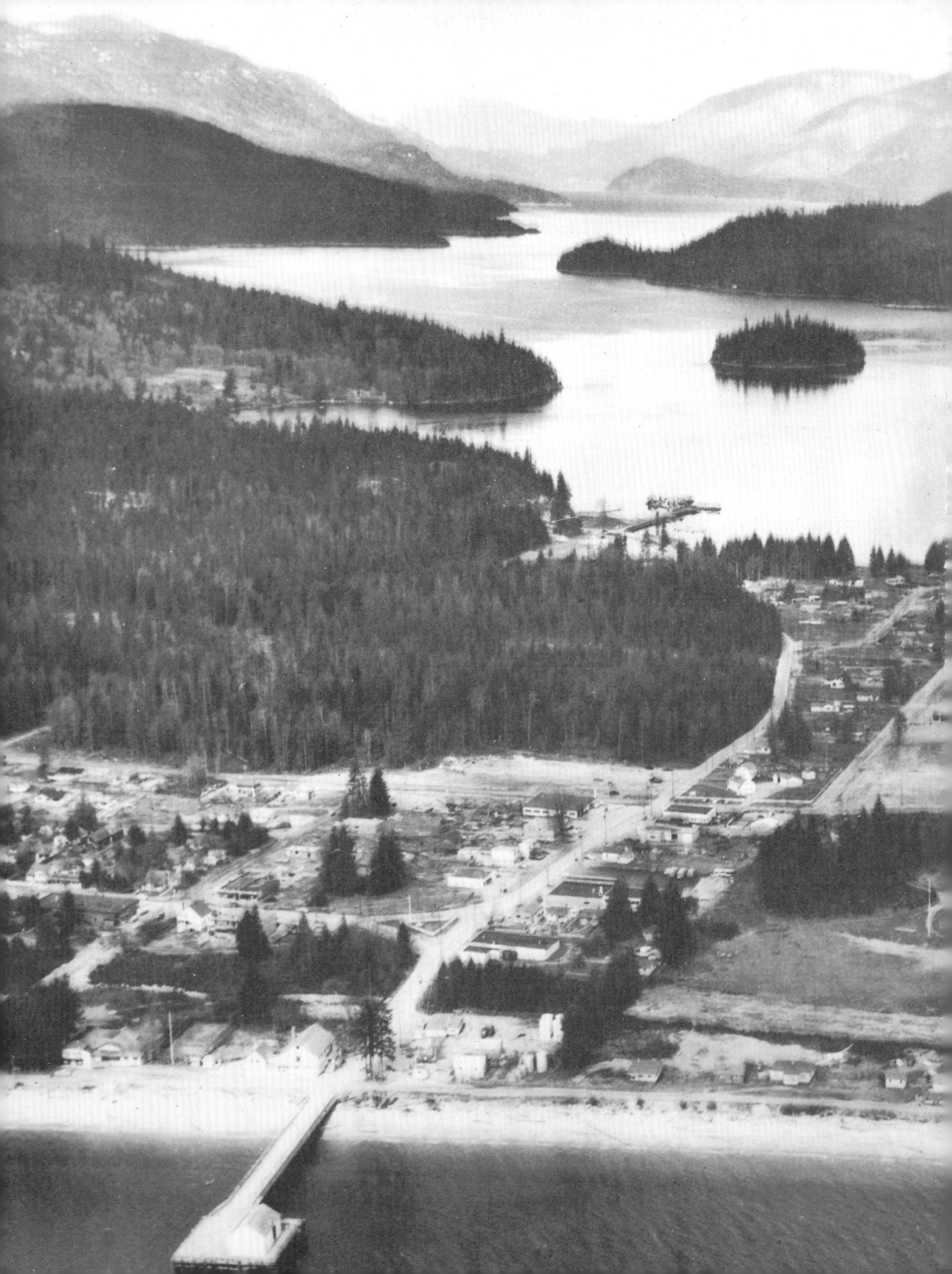